"If you or someone you know needs wise words to help reflect on life, purpose, meaning and God, look no further—this book is for you. Luke Cawley has carefully woven stories, examples, and questions into a tapestry that will spark fresh thinking on life's biggest questions. Whether you savour it in small bites on your daily commute or dive into it all at once in your favourite chair, I'm certain you'll find it an enriching and thought-provoking read."

TIM ADAMS, General Secretary, IFES

"No doubt all of us at times have an inkling that beyond the material and mundane features of life, perhaps even infused within them, lies something else. For those who are pilgrims on the search for meaning, or who are stumbling after God, *Somethingism* offers an earthy apologetic for taking a second look at the Christian story. Creatively written, and insightfully journeying through the realms of reason, intuition, and desire, *Somethingism* is a must-read for those trying to make sense of life's deepest questions."

DAN PATERSON, Founder and Speaker,
Questioning Christianity

"Curious and refreshingly personal, Luke takes us on a journey in this book from our rumbling sense that there might be something more towards the captivating possibility of a 'Someone' interested in knowing us."

BECCA NUNES, Arts Network Coordinator,
UCCF: The Christian Unions

T0343670

"Luke Cawley's book—one that needed to be written—points to the reality of a metaphysically haunted universe, and he invites us to explore what that is all about. Human beings commonly report about signs and indicators and their intuitions of an inescapable Something that is 'out there', and Cawley reminds us that this Something—the God who reveals himself in Jesus Christ—is not far from each one of us."

PAUL COPAN, Pledger Family Chair of Philosophy and Ethics, Palm Beach Atlantic University, FL; Author, *Loving Wisdom: A Guide to Philosophy and Christian Faith*

"Raw. Honest. Real. With unflinching authenticity, Luke Cawley guides readers through his own journey from 'something' to 'Someone', simultaneously inviting an exploration of God."

JEFF HOFFMEYER, Adjunct Professor, Fuller Theological Seminary

"It's so refreshing to read something by someone who obviously enjoys reading. This is clear throughout Luke's book—because in order to write well you need to read well, and he certainly writes well. The case being made is solid and clever, non-threatening and intriguing, but I particularly enjoyed rolling and ticking along on the back of the linguistic dexterity. This is a writer who knows his reader, knows himself and knows his métier. Lovely stuff, I'd say."

ANDY KIND, Comedian; Author, *Hidden in Plain Sight*

>Somethingism

+Exploring Our Sense of More

Luke Cawley

thegoodbook
COMPANY

Somethingism

© Luke Cawley, 2025

Published by:
The Good Book Company

thegoodbook.com | thegoodbook.co.uk
thegoodbook.com.au | thegoodbook.co.nz | thegoodbook.co.in

Cover design by Studio Gearbox | Art direction and design by André Parker

ISBN: 9781802543025 | JOB-008112 | Printed in India

"I walk slowly, like one who comes from so far away they don't expect to arrive."
Jorge Luis Borges

"He is not unknown because He is too far away, but because He is too close."
Tomáš Halík

To Whitney,
who is kind, thoughtful, insightful, witty and beautiful,
and for whom I am constantly thankful.

I said, "There is definitely some chemistry here,"
and then you, to my great relief, agreed.

Contents

Preface

This book came to life partly through conversations I've had about our sense that there may be more out there than we can see or touch—not necessarily a God but *something*. This intuition has been described by sociologists and others as "somethingism".[1] Somethingism is not a posture of commitment but simply of openness.

Some of my conversations about this have been private ones which arose naturally with friends as we each mused aloud. Others have been public—I work with a small non-profit, in a role which includes developing interactive events where participants can explore various big questions about life. These have been on university campuses, in schools, in theatres, and in a range of other locations.

Those present have brought a diverse range of questions and experiences to the room. And I can picture so many occasions when some of us have lingered to chat for hours after official event end times, or conversation has continued as we decamped to neighbouring pubs or eateries.

This book draws on the thinking these conversations have inspired, as well as my personal experience and some of the things I present at these events. It is offered to you as a way in which you might begin exploring your own sense of more.

And it starts with the story of your life.

Chapter One

The Story of Your Life

Everything comes into focus eventually. To begin with, though, it's just a blur of unfamiliar sound, bright light, and chilling air. We feel the skin of others against ours for the first time, as we are prodded, moved and bundled. Moments previously we were enveloped in darkness, warmth and the rhythmic throbbing of our mother's body. Nestled. Unaware of our own bodies and enshrouded in another's flesh.

Then this. In discomfort our lungs flood involuntarily with air, which we fire back out again in immediate protest—our wordless whimper entering the fray. Around us are faces. But we couldn't name them as such. Our eyes can scarcely settle on them. We've never seen anyone from the outside. Everything we encounter is unfamiliar and confusing.

Over following days, though, patterns emerge. This face, this smell, this voice—they herald sustenance, bring reassurance, relieve our disquiet. We feel settled by their presence. Some of the sounds, it soon emerges, signify us. Our name. We begin by turning our heads, later smiling, then laughing, as we hear it spoken. Each new mode of response evoking delight from those around us.

Forming the names of others becomes one of our tricks. Mama. Dada. Before long we can use our mouths to describe, identify, request, refuse, decry, appeal, acclaim and affirm. Once we sank teeth into our own toes and cried out in pain, unaware they were attached. Now we not only know they are ours, but we can use them to crawl, to stand, to kick.

Objects around us, previously little more than shapes, progressively assume meaning. Those vibrantly coloured sticks, with their waxy taste, are crayons. They leave marks on paper. And on walls, leading to tears and consequences. These glossy cardboard blocks, with chewed corners—books—open out to display pictures, and stories, and the small black shapes on them are a code we can learn, stuttering out the syllables, pushing forth the words, cracking open the story.

As we read, and interpret, and use words—spoken, read or written—we begin to piece things together. There was a world which preceded us. Kings and queens, empires and wars, exploration and discovery, enslavement and liberation. We exist in a continuum. In musty classrooms we are briefed on past findings— gravity, electricity, combustion, cells, atoms, vaccines. Great artists, writers, and musicians dance into the frame. Passions and interests are inflamed. Tastes refined. Ambitions inaugurated.

We learn to manipulate tools in pursuit of these desires. Not only paintbrushes and pencils but screens and keyboards. Objects built for communication. Decades later we may wryly reminisce at the items we once considered innovative, just as we now smile as *we* picture *our* forebears marvelling at the town's first motorcar, or inviting neighbours to watch their colour television, or spinning a dial on their hallway telephones. Our generation's most ubiquitous technologies are glowing pocketable bricks of glass and metal, which travel with us as we login, message, post, share, like and upload.

Content and mode of expression can—we learn—affect others, both on these devices and in person. It can advance our standing in the school, the family, the social network. Friendships can be strengthened or destroyed, made toxic or infused with life, by the choices we make. Through observation and imitation, and by failure and success, we progressively refine the selves we present to the world, and the self we aspire to become.

Guiding us are people like parents and peers, yes, but also ideas. Some are studied at school—"All [people] are created equal", "The history of all ... society is the history of class struggles", and the dream "that one day people will not be judged by the colour of their skin but by the content of their character".[2] Others come embedded in our entertainment—"Be true to yourself", "One day my love will come", "Follow your heart".[3] Still more arrive on our social-media feed—"Don't cry because it finished, smile because it happened", "It always seems impossible until it's done", and "The key to success is failure".[4] We rotate them between the fingers of our minds; adopting, adapting and rejecting.

Seeking what works, coheres and helps us navigate our existence.

Until, eventually, we are launched out, no longer living under the supervision of those who raised us—although their imprint is never completely erased. And we continue our unfurling. Moving, communicating, consuming, interpreting, learning, choosing, deliberating. Taking all we have encountered in days past, and reapplying it today, and in days to come. As, slowly, more of our surroundings—and even of ourselves—comes into focus.

How It Started, How It's Going

To become who you are today required all that came before. From your instinctual first breath to everything that has happened over the past year, your capacity to learn, adapt and reskill has been essential. It is to your benefit that you acquired language, became mobile, gained familiarity with the alphabet, encountered the art and stories of others, became adept with technology, refined your ability to relate to others, and developed values to inform your choices.

None of us idealises an incapacity to grow. We don't ordinarily wish we had less understanding or fewer skills, or that we had remained crawling and gurgling, dependent on others to change our underwear. It has served us well to be curious and inquisitive people, open to future discoveries. And we're not done learning yet. Every time you ask a question of someone or search for something online, you are admitting to the existence of the unknown—to the possibility of things outside your current frame of understanding.

Our growth as people can be summarised in two simple words. The first is "experience". As we have developed over the years, we have encountered new people, situations, and items, increasing how much of reality we have experienced. We all also know that there are aspects of reality that we simply haven't yet experienced. At the time of writing, for example, I have never explored a coral reef. It lies outside my own frame of lived experience. Some elements of known reality, in fact, don't just sit beyond the reach of individual people but of humanity as a whole—the surface of Mars, for example, remains for now both real and untouched by human feet.

Alongside "experience", consider the word "perception". It is quite possible for a person to *experience* something but not *perceive* it. I was licking books for some time before I perceived the meaning of the words on the page. We often assume that if something is important and real, then it will be obvious to us. But many things can happen without us perceiving them. We might not perceive that the pickpocket on the bus is targeting us. But when we get home and find he has emptied our bank account, we wish we had perceived more clearly.

When speaking to university students on this subject as part of my work, I often ask them to imagine that there is someone in their class who would be their ideal life partner. And "More than this," I add, "they are already attracted to you. They think about you day and night. A melting sensation crosses their chest whenever they glimpse you; but you haven't noticed, and they've never said anything. Here is a potentially life-altering experience—spending every day in a lecture hall with a well-suited person who adores you—which remains unperceived."

To navigate life, then, requires both experiencing the new and also perceiving more clearly those things which are *already* a part of our experience. The scientist and philosopher Michael Polanyi, who wrote extensively on how we grow in understanding, described knowledge not as something we receive passively but as the product of us fitting the pieces together, staring at it all until, over time (and probably with the help of others), we begin to perceive the patterns and connections.[5]

One of Polanyi's interpreters compares this to gazing at a magic-eye picture: those abstract pieces of art which have embedded in them an image not visible from a brief cursory look.[6] As we attempt to focus our eyes just past the page, a three-dimensional shape, placed there by the artist, becomes so clear that we can now barely avoid it. It was always present, but now it has become visible *to us*.

One of the temptations as we grow older is to cease staring at reality—to operate on the basis of patterns already perceived and experiences already acquired. This, to an extent, is quite reasonable. I expect you can get through tomorrow perfectly competently without any monumental paradigm shifts. You can speak, move and count, and can operate all the technology you need—not to mention handling (most) basic human relationships. And yet, for many of us, there remains a subtle and persistent sense that possibly not *everything* crucial has yet come into focus—that perhaps there's something more that lies beyond our current experience or evades our consistent perception.

The Fluttering Wings

Sometimes this sense flutters into the very periphery of our inner vision, faintly flickering there for a moment like the beating wings of a passing bird, providing us with a fleeting impression that there is something more to life. Yet when we turn our heads towards the blur of light, it is gone. So we can neither name what we glimpsed nor deny its passing presence.

Perhaps, for example, you've had that experience of staring up at the stars on a clear night and being doused in an intense awareness of your own smallness, and the great swathes of reality you cannot know. In that moment your current perspectives on life feel more like tentative working theories than settled conclusions. Maybe there really are "more things in heaven and earth," as Shakespeare's Hamlet said, "than are dreamt of in your philosophy".[7]

Gazing into the night sky—at these objects so far away—we become pierced by the possibility that all that it means to be human, to be us, is not found in our immediate surroundings and present experiences.[8] It stirs in us an urge towards something greater, and for a time anything, even—dare we say it—God, becomes a slightly less outlandish proposition. Not that we would want to necessarily be so specific as to say "God". But at least, perhaps, the transcendent: a *something* or *someone*, more than material, who *is* and whose paths intersect, be it ever so occasionally, with our own.

A friend of mine says she had no real interest in these kinds of questions until she was listening to a piece of music, and she became so overwhelmed by the beauty of it that for the first time she found herself asking, "What if there is a God, or something like that?" Art, literature and film can all at times provoke this sensation. The novelist Iris Murdoch writes that "art pierces the veil and gives sense to the notion of a reality which lies beyond appearance".[9] Perhaps it has had a similar effect for you. It opened you up to something indefinable.

Yet this sense of something more doesn't necessarily come to us in punctuated moments of acute clarity. For some of us, it can just kind of linger in the background. The astronomer Galileo described it as something he encountered in the process of his scientific endeavours, commenting that mathematics is the language with which God wrote the universe—the order and harmony of the cosmos seemed to him like glimpses of the divine.[10]

For others it can be still less specific. Singer-songwriter Regina Spektor, best known for the title song to *Orange Is the New Black*, told an interviewer that this sense is something which "I've always had ... like, kind of naturally".[11] Intuition tells her that we can't reduce reality down to what we can see or touch or measure. We, and our partners, friends and children—each is more than the sum of their biological processes and chemical composition.

Our little world feels awash with the subtlest of whispers in this direction. Philosopher Tomáš Halík says that many of us today subscribe to "somethingism"; we "don't believe in God ... don't go to church, but [we] know there is *something* above us".[12] Our persistent sense of "*something*" more remains unshakeable, even if we are loathe to attach any particular definition to it.

Others of us, though, are struck less by the *presence* of the transcendent than its perceived *absence*. There seems to be a brutality and darkness to the world that crushes any possibility of God or similar concepts. And yet, strangely, even this sense of God's absence doesn't eliminate the question of whether there is more. An atheist friend once told me that he lies in bed every night staring at the ceiling and asks himself, "Is this it?" We can be as haunted by the impression that there is nothing as we can by those recurring intuitions of something. At least if there is a God, you can rail against them for all that's going on. If, though, we live in a universe which one writer described as having "at bottom, no design, no purpose, no evil, no good, nothing but blind, pitiless indifference", then you really don't have anyone towards whom to even shake a fist.[13]

The most intriguing moments for many of us are when we come across others who seem to have moved from simply *perceiving* the possibility of something more to consistently embracing it. These are people who would say that the unseen dimension—the transcendent—is an integrated part of their ongoing life story. They might be prominent individuals that we see from a distance or in history lessons—like the Dalai Lama, Bishop Desmond Tutu, or educational campaigner Malala Yousafzai—or someone we stumbled across on their social-media channel.

But more likely it is those populating our daily existence who provoke us to ponder: the friends, family members and co-workers who we know firsthand to be intelligent, rational, honest people who, nevertheless, drop hints of a spiritual aspect to their lives. When you're going through a difficult time, they say, "I'll pray for you", and it seems like more than a platitude. Perhaps they even straight-up claim that God is a part of their everyday. They've even told you some of their story and experience in that area. Not that you would buy into their whole system or credit their every explanation. Nor are you exactly sure that their experience is for people like you. But they do seem to have something which you don't. It's, at the very least, good *for them*. There are plenty of people who use religion and spirituality as a pretext to be a jerk, but *this* person isn't in that category, and that raises some questions.

And so, woven into our lives is a sense that more is going on than we perceive. This possibility flutters indefinably around the perimeters of our perception— capturing our attention fully at particular moments while at other times fading almost completely into the shadowy corners of our consciousness. Even when we feel most alone in the world, the question still presses upon us, "Is this it?"—or even more pointedly, "To whom do I direct my frustration and discontent?" Will everything really come into focus eventually?

>Pause and Consider (or Discuss)

1. Do you ever have a sense that there's something more? What has given you that sense?

2. If there is some transcendent aspect of reality, or even a God, do you think you have either (1) experienced or (2) perceived this at that some point? When and how?

3. Do you know anyone who seems to you like a spiritual person, or someone who has "something" you don't? What is it about them that gives you this impression?

Chapter Two

Starting
> Somewhere

Like trying to hug a cloud. That's the best way I can describe it. Throwing my arms around the object of my attention, only to find them passing frictionless through the vapour. Every day, I would wander through the park, pausing on the same isolated bench for around an hour, reaching towards *whoever* or *whatever* was out there, only to again return home dissatisfied, eluded.

Ever since I was quite small, I'd had the sense that there was something more than the physical or material and with which, or whom, I could connect. It was like fluttering wings at the periphery of my vision—so I attempted to bring them into focus. As I walked and sat each day I would, in turns, both talk aloud—you might call it praying—and then lapse into silence, awaiting... well, what did I want? Some kind of reciprocity. Not a voice but at least an incremental heightening of clarity as to what was out there. An increased sense of closeness.

Even a simple first step towards exploring our sense of more, like trying to "think about God", can be frustratingly elusive. Ambiguity rushes in from the moment we attempt to sketch even a basic outline of what we mean by "God". On the bench it always felt to me as if I was trying to direct my thoughts outwards towards some invisible object, all the time hoping that I was projecting them in the appropriate direction. A kind of psychological contortion act in which it was unclear if I was simply manipulating myself.

One of my friends, in his days as a religious-affairs journalist, was covering a press conference in a crypt, held by a future British prime minister. As people began their post-event dispersal, he sidled up to the politician and raised the question of God. "What," he asked, "is your take?" The man looked shocked and exclaimed, "Are you actually asking me what I believe?" He ran his hand through his hair, hemmed for a moment, and then replied, "I'd say I believe, but it's like trying to get a radio signal when you're driving through the Chilterns"—a particularly hilly area of central England. "Sometimes you can get it, and sometimes you can't, and you're just left twiddling the dial."[14]

Many of us can relate. I know I would sometimes come away from the park feeling as though I had been in the presence of another—though those moments often crept up on me unexpectedly, and more through the silences than my words. Most often I was left to provide my own etchings on the meaning of "God". I was like the multicultural class of children that a friend once asked to draw a picture of God. The Japanese boy drew a samurai, the Americans pictured him in jeans, and the others in their local costumes. We so easily sketch a God in our own image.[15]

Maybe God was angry, dissatisfied, benevolent, loving, or even just indifferent. My understanding of whatever was out there fluctuated with my mood as much as anything else. It was also besieged by questions about how, as a rational person, I could continue believing in something like God. I knew there was a vast number of people who spoke of God intelligently and thoughtfully—a list which these days would range from friends and family through to writers like Donna Tartt and Marilynne Robinson, scientists like Kizzmekia Corbett and Francis Collins, and artists and musicians such as Makoto Fujimura and Lauren Daigle.[16] A gnawing sense persisted, though, that there was something slightly antiquated about the whole business: that humanity as a whole, and I personally, needed to move on from this.

But I couldn't. Actually, I tried, and it resolved less than you'd imagine. I told God, "I don't think you exist, and if you do exist, I don't like you". Visits to the bench faded away, and my increased distancing from God felt faintly liberating, though it hardly remedied anything— all of us, regardless of our perspective on "something", have to navigate the same world, and very few issues are dispelled simply by waving God away. But, like many people, I could live with a blend of scepticism and distaste towards whatever or whoever was out there.

Then, just as I thought I'd moved on, a parcel arrived and gave me pause to think again. In it was a book I'd asked my mum to buy some time previously, which touched on the topic of the transcendent.[17] It described what many people mean when they say "God", and its definition reframed some of my experiences in the park and reanimated my curiosity towards encountering this *something*. God became, through that book and my subsequent investigations, less of an intangible cloud and more of a tantalising possibility.

God, the Universe and Everything

God, it turns out, is not a thing. Nor is God a being. But this does not mean God is not real. When the word "God" is used with a clear definition, it is usually either by academic philosophers, theologians or by people with specific religious convictions—say, Muslims, Christians or Jews. And it ordinarily designates the source of all reality: less *a thing* than that without which there would be no*thing*—less *a being* than *the ground of all being*.[18]

God, as a concept, communicates that we and all we experience are contingent on something other than ourselves. When talking about God, I often like to draw a circle, to represent the universe, and then to write the word "us" inside the shape and "God" beyond its exterior. Then I mark some lines indicating that God, while continuing to somehow relate to our reality, is not just another item on the inventory of objects found in our reality.[19]

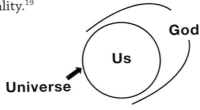

God is not like cheese or trees or neural circuits or dark matter or democracy. We cannot hope to find God nor to prove or disprove God's existence—at least, not through our own investigative capacities. Some people say that science has dispelled God, and others say that it does quite the opposite. But actually, on this understanding of God, science—a discipline focused on the contents of our universe—is a mistaken direction for the conversation. Because God is not some element *in* the circle. It's not as if we might someday unscrew the appropriate cosmic panel and behind it find God, beavering away, keeping the whole thing going. Nor are we going to stumble across irrefutable evidence of his non-existence.

Columbia University physicist Brian Greene, commenting on the usefulness of science to the God question, says:

> *"Science only has something to say about a very particular notion of God, which goes by the name of 'God of the gaps': if you are trying to understand the world around you and science has not yet given an explanation for some phenomenon, you could step back and say, 'Oh, that is God.' Then, when science does explain that phenomena—as it eventually does—God gets squeezed out because he is no longer needed to explain that phenomena. But that is a very particular and simplistic notion of God. No matter what physics does, you can always say there is God behind it: God set up the rules [for] the physics, God set the environment within which those rules play themselves out."* [20]

God, then, is not a thing in the circle at which we can clutch or a cheap explanation for our gaps in knowledge. He is not a cog in the wheels of the Big Bang, evolution, the movements of the planets, or any other physical process—though, without him, none of these things would exist, and nor would we.

Yet neither is he some distant abstraction. If there is a God, a non-material source of all that exists, then we all inhabit the very reality he generated. To be alive is therefore to experience God. "In him we live and move and have our being", as the ancient philosophers wrote, and so "he is not far from any one of us".[21] As those whose existence is made possible only by something outside ourselves, we—with our every contingent breath—inescapably brush up against the divine simply by *being*. There is no special action required on our part. It is therefore unsurprising that, as slippery as this something more may prove, we find ourselves unshakeably haunted by its possibility.

God can only come into focus, though, if he reveals himself—providing clarity *within* our reality. God—or something along those lines—has, many of us intuit, been part of our experience, even at the corners of our perception. But we cannot pierce beyond the proverbial circle to gain a clearer glimpse. It requires his self-disclosure within our universe for us to know him with any precision. He must take the initiative to show himself to us.

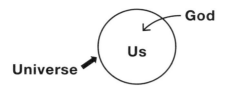

We, as humans, are creatures bound to time and place, and if God were to make himself known with accentuated clarity, then he would need to do so at unique local points—and through specific things—*within* our space-time experience. Otherwise he would remain inaccessible to us. One key question, then, is whether he has done this: has God revealed himself within the circle? If he has, then it is by attending to those moments and places of self-disclosure that our own sense of something more can edge away from cloud-like nebulousness and towards tangible reality.

Starting Somewhere

Searching for God is, like much else in life, a dance between the general and the particular. We become gripped every day by broad desires—hunger, relaxation, learning, love, to name a few—which we seek to fulfil through specific means. Our aching abdomens lead us to *this* Indian restaurant, where we select *that* dish; our tired bodies throw themselves down before *one* Netflix show, not all of them at once; our curious minds purchase *a number* of books, but not the entire contents of the bookstore. Our wish for a life partner leads us to begin conversations, go to places where we might meet someone, or sign up for apps and websites which enable us to initiate contact with individual people.

General desires without particular actions tend to remain unfulfilled. A hungry man who eschews ever biting on any specific food will starve. An inquisitive woman who never reads a book will be stunted in her learning. The lonely student who refuses human contact will likely remain single. We move from the general ("I hope there's *someone* out there for me") to the particular ("I'll have a drink with *this* person and see if it might be them"). We don't make this move because we are narrow or arrogant or closed-minded, but precisely because the *only* way to respect the general is not to submerge it in formaldehyde for display on the shelf—all the time preserving our broad sense of being people interested in *this kind of thing*—but to act upon it by exploring particular possible avenues for its fulfilment.

It's similar when we come to the transcendent, to the spiritual or to God. To make sense of this question we have to start *somewhere*: we step from the general sense that God—or something similar—could be there, and towards the specific concrete affirmations that people today make about the transcendent. Most people who would describe God as part of their everyday experience don't only believe that he has left hints in the world around us, but also that he has somehow also brought himself into sharp focus at identifiable moments and locations within the "circle" of human history. Our capacity to grapple with the concept of God will, as in other areas of life, depend partly on whether we are willing to pause and consider these specifics.

Which feels daunting. There are often assumed to be thousands of options when it comes to the question of God; selecting one is a far more complex undertaking than satiating your hunger through choosing between a balti and a jalfrezi on the takeaway menu. And yet, while it is true that there are many affirmations about the transcendent, relatively few of them have ever gained traction beyond their geographical and ethnic points of origin. There are lots of ideas, yes—but not many which are taken seriously by large numbers of people today. Which, surely, is a good place to start—by asking what others around the globe are finding both works for them and is credible. Not because truth is established by popular vote but simply because, if you are going to ask a big question like the possibility of God, then you can assume that other thinking people are already on the case, and, at the very least, you may want to take a glance at their findings.

The widespread options, it turns out, are few. There are just seven ways of approaching the transcendent which are currently affirmed by more than one percent of the world's population: Buddhism, atheism/agnosticism, Hinduism, Chinese traditional religion, African traditional religion, Islam, and Christianity.[22] Variety abounds within each one, and overlap occurs between them, but they at least provide a starting point.[23]

It could be that none of these seven are true. Perhaps the reality of God is known only to a solitary old lady living alone in a remote Peruvian village, and this knowledge will soon die with her. But if we are adequately to dance from the general to the particular, then humility suggests that, while allowing for the Peruvian-pensioner possibility, we also need to step in for a closer look at one or more of these seven claims. Indeed, if the transcendent is calling to us, inviting us towards itself (or even herself or himself: the personal pronouns suggesting that the source of our reality has a mind and will rather than indicating a specific identifiable gender), then it would be strange to pre-emptively dismiss those and assume that this "something" is ours alone to discover.

Not that the destination is religion exactly. Our longing for more doesn't feel, for most of us, like something which can be satisfied by religion—not, at least, as we may have experienced it until now; the cheery vicars, strange statues, bizarre rules, arcane scriptures and violent, irresolvable conflicts all seem quite detached from our own interests and, we intuit, also those of God. We are, instead, as one writer put it, like those born remembering music they have never heard.[24] At our very core we find a restlessness to hear that tune again—somewhere far beyond ritual, and directly from the source.

Religion cannot fulfil this desire. Neither can non-religion. Something deeper is calling to us. Yet, perhaps, particular elements conventionally associated with religion can help our response. Those who peer more intently into these popular claims about God frequently find themselves surprised. They often discover something more profound than a ritualistic superstructure or an ethical code. Instead, they stumble across a reality which is both compelling and, at moments, unsettling. But it doesn't always lie on the surface.

If we pause any initial instinct towards dismissiveness, then, we may begin to better perceive whatever is drawing us. Tomáš Halík, whose work provides the inspiration for this book's title, has suggested that the experience of God hinges on our patience.[25] God may not be immediately obvious, he says, but those who are willing to slowly explore, rather than rapidly dash elsewhere, reap the rewards. This process, though, may unfold best when it has as its focus a particular perspective on God.

This was true for me. On the bench and in the park, I did all I could to reach out and open myself up toward whatever was behind my general sense of something more. I committed countless hours to breaking through: pushing past the hints and rumours of God's existence and towards something more enduring. It proved beyond me; God wasn't apprehendable solely by my own efforts in prayer and meditation, so I walked away. Only when a book arrived, the contents of which drew my eye from the general and towards the particular, did the impenetrability begin to fade. God slid from nebulous cloud to tangible reality.

Over the coming chapters, we will consider the specific way of looking at the transcendent that helped me. Perhaps, as we do so, things will also come into focus for you. As with all else in life though, we have to start somewhere. We dance from the general to the particular and begin our journey there.

>Pause and Consider (or Discuss):

1. What images or ideas typically come to your mind when you think of the word "God"?

2. Have you ever tried to reach out to God (or whatever/whoever is out there), whether by prayer, meditation, or other means? What was your experience?

3. With what specific claims about God making himself known are you most familiar? What most attracts you to these claims, and what pushes you away?

Chapter Three

Accessible
> and Escapable

God could come to us as a formula—a complex and involved equation. Our greatest minds would huddle around their supercomputers, assistants dashing chalk across the blackboard as algorithms are cracked and complexities unravelled. They might build a machine, immense and housed in a valley within some obscure European microstate. Vast quantities of energy would be absorbed to enable calculations far beyond the capacities of the human mind until, finally, it would be solved. In that moment we would know beyond all doubt the reality of God and his message for us.

Or it could be to philosophers that he makes himself accessible. Through a string of logical propositions, agreed ideas balanced one upon the next, we would see that—yes—God is not only logically unavoidable but his qualities and nature, his purposes with humankind, all make sense to anyone with the appropriate rational capacities to grasp them. Then we could memorise these arguments and use them to present God to anyone willing to engage their minds.

Maybe God could reveal himself not through a proposition but a substance. A plant perhaps. Possibly a flower. When it was placed in our house, we would glimpse his beauty. Meditating upon it would open our minds to his reality. Its petals could be dried and crushed, then imbibed—eaten, smoked, injected, or inhaled—creating an experience of intense clarity. Then, riding that high, we would feel what God is.

Or he could give us a ritual. A series of actions we perform. Maybe in a sacred place. Arranging the pieces, uttering the appropriate words, clutching the artefacts, as our participation in the rehearsed drama conveys to us the shape of God himself. We'd enter in ignorance, but as we took these ancient steps, we would soon leave in secure knowledge.

God could easily leave us in no doubt: with no requirement to search or question. Each morning as we eat our breakfast, his voice could thunder from the skies: "Just to remind you that there is a God, and I am he". Or you could close your eyes, and there, etched inside your eyelids in bright lights, would be your daily message from God: "I love you", "Try harder", "I'm actually not that interested in you", "Don't forget your lunchbox", or whatever it was he wanted to say. Such means would leave us with no doubt that he existed and no question about what he wished to convey.

How God reveals himself, if indeed he does so at all, will shape the way we encounter him. Logical means, like equations and propositions, would be certain and convincing. Yet also impersonal and distant. Yes, they might spell out that he existed and even what he had to say. But he would essentially be a fact that we could memorize and print in textbooks. And even the most attractive of mathematical formulae is relatively unengaging for the majority—very few of us glow with excitement at the words "Let's do some algebra".

Physical means, like foods or substances, would make for a more intimate encounter. God would be known through a sensation or a feeling. Intensity could be possible. Voices from the sky, or lights on our eyelids, could add even more clarity. God would become inescapable, like the existence of the sun, gravity or the wind. We'd have to take him into account, and we would have no room for manoeuvre when questioned on his existence.

While some of these examples are sketched in outlandish terms, they do represent a few of the expectations we might have of God—that he could be encountered as a feeling, an idea, the sensations of a religious or spiritual ritual, or as an unavoidable voice speaking from the clouds. On one level this makes sense; if God is the source of all reality, as I suggested in the previous chapter, then we would likely find echoes of him in everything, from our rationality to our emotions, rituals and physical sensations. But what if the *clearest* way he has communicated himself is not through any of these things but something altogether more intriguing?

What if God has come to us humans through the most relatable means possible—as a person, walking among us, living out a life story which, like ours, stretches from messy birth to uninvited death? If this were so, then we would access the reality of God not through reasoning our way towards him, nor by discovering a physical item or rite which unlocked the truth, and still less by tuning our emotions into the appropriate frequency. Instead, we would contemplate this person and, in the process, glimpse the face of God himself. As we did so, we would begin understanding what—indeed, *who*—is behind the sense that there is something more.

Knowing People

People are the basic components of our lives. Most days are constructed from a series of interpersonal encounters—banter with workmates, gossip from the hairdresser, avoided eye contact with the shopkeeper, likes and messages from our social-media contacts, meals and stories with the family, or evenings with the other half. We might find ourselves fuming at an email from our child's teacher, worrying about the health of an ageing relative, reeling in pain from the betrayal of an assumed ally, or even just losing ourselves in a book or film which relays the fictional events of an invented character's life.

If God has come to us as a person, then he has chosen a means which is intuitively accessible. We know people because we are people. Another person, however strange they might be, is always "one of us"—they have bodies which resemble ours, along with desires, memories, choices, friendships, parents, reputations, ambitions and priorities, just as we do. People can be frustrating, though, and even unsettling; very few of us lie awake at night reflecting on how a philosophical proposition or religious ritual has not come through for us in our time of need. We have expectations of people which are dissimilar to those we have towards any other element in world.

From the moment we meet another person, we measure them by how they speak and treat us, and the stories others tell about them. What little objectivity we had quickly begins to fade. Analysing a personal acquaintance as one would a chemical compound is impossible—once we share the same space and open our mouths, they become a part of our story and not simply an external object. And yet, for all this familiarity, they remain curiously beyond final definition. Even our closest friends always extend beyond our field of vision; we *know* specific people, yes, and yet we are simultaneously in the process of *getting to know* them better. They are not solvable like an escape room, and we cannot complete someone as we would a video game or a mathematical puzzle.

Nobody comes home from a night out and announces to their flatmates, "I met the most wonderful person on earth; I'm glad I can mark that off my bucket list and move on with life". Instead, our encounters with others compel us to want to know them better, to arrange a second meeting, to more deeply entwine our existence with theirs—or, at times, to begin disentangling ourselves when we glimpse some dark, hidden aspect of their character. There is, therefore, always an element of questioning in every relationship. We can never have 100% certitude regarding what we perceive or experience in another.

People, then, do not offer an undoubtable form of knowledge. We can, though, be sufficiently confident in specific others to trust them, and even come to shape some of our life decisions around conversations we have and promises we make to one another. It is not irrational to do so but simply a different way of knowing and deciding than through statements, ideas, consumable substances and collective rituals. Human relationship is complementary to these other means of understanding the world, and even intersects with them at points but remains a distinct and unique experience.

For most of us, it is in relationships that we make sense even of ourselves. If our parents loved us unconditionally, then we will more likely see ourselves as suitable objects of another's affections. If they abused us then we may grow to view ourselves differently. Our peer groups likewise shape us—perhaps we began on the social fringe at school, conditioned to see ourselves as hopeless oddballs, only to later stumble across a new set of friends who recognised us as someone interesting with innate value. It is through others that we often find our own footing.

It was this perspective on God which helped me begin to make sense of my intuition that there is something more out there: namely, that he has shown himself to us in the life of a human—a compelling, frustrating, uncontrollable person like us, whom we can both know and get to know, all the time helping us orient ourselves to ourselves. The specific person was Jesus of Nazareth, whose silhouetted image appeared on the cover of the book I mentioned in the previous chapter. He said things like "Whoever has seen me has seen [God]" and, "I and [God] are one".[26] The implication being that he provides us with a concentrated and focused glimpse of the transcendent. God, according to Jesus, has a human face and a life story, and it is his own.

If this is accurate and Jesus shows us God, then the stories of his life become crucial. A number of early biographies of him, eyewitness accounts from his 1st-century acquaintances, remain widely available today.[27] These texts are the most detailed and vivid portraits of Jesus ever recorded, and continue to define how he is understood around the world. Accessing them simply requires reading or listening. Glimpsing the transcendent, on this account, is much like curling up with a good book: an experience which, like human relationships, can be involving, frustrating, and transformative.

The historical distance between these texts and our time is less significant than we might assume—the idea here is not that God *was* like the character on their pages but that he *still is* this way. There is a continuity between who we encounter in these narratives and the something that we sense is out there, fluttering at the periphery of our perception. Jesus himself said, "I am the door", and the stories of him are not intended as an end in themselves but instead to swing open for us both an understanding and an experience of God, moving us beyond the nebulous sense of embracing a cloud and towards something more tangible and enduring.[28]

Escapably Accessible

Between curiosity and openness is where most relationships begin. Something about a person piques our interest—maybe it's looks, reputation, a comment or sense of connection, or even just our own restless urge to explore. And from there we choose to spend time together, in person and virtually, regularly turning over the possibilities in our minds. We rarely jump to instant commitment. But neither do we make our deliberations in isolation from the object of our curiosity. We instead quite naturally assume that proximity to them might afford more clarity than distance would.

Human beings, though, are also evadable. We can easily go cold on them or even withdraw completely. Ghosting, the phenomenon of completely severing all contact unannounced, is commonplace. People may be compelling and capable of getting under our skin, but they can also be given a wide berth when we choose to do so. There are millions of people in your country, thousands in your locale, and yet you have close connections with only a few of them.

God, if he has come to us as a person, is similarly ghostable. Jesus, for example, is probably the best-known individual in human history and a continued object of fascination for those of all religious persuasions and none—a prophet in Islam, an avatar or projection of the divine for numerous Hindus, and a fully-enlightened bodhisattva for many Buddhists.[29] And for countless agnostic or atheistic artists and writers—from Frida Kahlo and Hannah Arendt to Philip Pullman and José Saramago—he remains a muse and enigma.[30] There is something unshakeably intriguing about this man, which keeps catching the eye far beyond the boundaries of the Christian movement which he initiated or his native Jewish context, within which he was a rabbi and wandering storyteller.[31] And yet, if you want to go years—or even a lifetime—without giving him serious consideration, you can easily do so.

It's almost as if we have to choose to look. Mathematician Blaise Pascal wrote of God that "there is enough light for those who want to see, and enough shadow for those who want to hide".[32] We can, Pascal affirms, ghost God. Or we can step in for a closer look. We don't do the latter from a position of commitment; instead, as we might with other people, we approach him with a combination of curiosity and openness, both of which can coexist with caution and even healthy scepticism.

Over the coming chapters, we'll begin to consider this *particular* claim of God's self-disclosure in a human life story. If God has shown himself in the character and narrative of Jesus, then he has come to us in a form which is intriguing, relatable, evadable and—crucially— accessible and investigable. "You don't have to bring a thing to it," writes novelist Marilynne Robinson, "except a little willingness to see".[33]

>Pause and Consider (or Discuss)

1. What life story or biography has most shaped you—whether it was someone telling your their story first-hand or through written or film versions? In what ways did it do so?

2. Have you ever had the experience of feeling that your friendship with another person has helped you make sense of yourself... or left you more confused? What happened?

3. If God has shown himself through the life and person of a particular individual in history, what about that would you find attractive, and what questions would it raise?

Chapter Four

Reframing the
> **Something**

Earthiness marked his life from the beginning. He was conceived in a small village where occupying soldiers mixed with resentful locals, before a government edict forced his parents—his mother heavily pregnant—to relocate to the city, where he was born in a home, most likely, of some distant relatives.[34] We know little of his life there except that, while he was still a toddler, his family scrambled out of town under cover of darkness right before a government-sanctioned massacre ripped through the streets they had just vacated.[35]

A period as refugees in North Africa was followed by a return to the village where scandalous rumours around his parentage still swirled. His name, Jesus, was the local version of Joshua, referencing a famous liberator of his nation in centuries long passed, and his mother even composed a song during her pregnancy about how her son would topple the powerful and exalt the poor and downtrodden. But he seemed far from such a revolutionary leader for his first three decades. Instead, he followed in his father's occupation as a member of the building trade: a carpenter probably helping craft the frames of various houses in surrounding settlements.

Somewhere along the line, his father fades from the historical narrative, presumably having died during Jesus' teenage years. Meanwhile, his cousin John—an influential local figure who drew massive crowds to hear his fiery oratory, and would soon be arrested and executed by local authorities—publicly pointed a finger in Jesus' direction and designated him as one sent by God to do something decisive in the world. Jesus then disappeared for over a month, wandering in the wilderness, and on his return quit the building trade to follow in his cousin's footsteps as a travelling teacher.

His family seemed less than impressed. Likewise his neighbours: he triggered a riot in his village after being invited to speak at the local synagogue. His message there suggested that God's priorities might not align with his listeners' nationalistic ambitions but—instead—that God loves and embraces all peoples. His audience, discerning the intended implication that this love extends even to members of the occupying military forces, sought to murder him by attempting to throw him from a nearby cliff, only for him to slip away.

Thereafter he traversed the nation with a group of followers or apprentices—a model of student travelling companions popular with both Greek philosophers and Jewish rabbis. Jesus, though, selected as his followers a strange mix of local small businessmen, a dodgy civil servant, a member of a revolutionary terrorist band, and others with backgrounds so nondescript that they don't even merit a description in the historical record. None were from the social or economic elite. Nor were any recognised as religious leaders. They didn't have accents indicative of high education, nor did any of them sound like an earnest young clergyperson. Opening their mouths revealed a distinctly local twang which invoked mockery from the ruling classes—surely, they laughed, God could not be working through someone whose entourage sounded *like this*. Some knew of Jesus' family and asked exactly who this man—Josh the builder, son of Joe the builder, from some rural backwater— thought that he was.

His aggravation of the authorities, though, was mirrored by explosive acclaim among the disempowered. The stories of his life are punctuated by interactions with those on the fringes of society—those with reputations as immoral or untrustworthy, people crushed by the system, burdened by life. They turned out in their thousands. Consistent disregard for respectability marked his selection of conversation partners, and he refused to turn anyone away, even going so far as to physically embrace those known to have infectious skin diseases, and publicly welcoming local sex workers to the dining table.

Stories were his preferred mode of communication. Jesus forged meaning through metaphor, simile and dramatic action.[36] He operated more like a playwright or poet than a philosopher. Miniature verbal dramas were stitched from everyday items like economic crises, building projects, lost possessions, agricultural practices, family breakdowns and shady employers. From these relatable elements, he forged tales which are retold to this day.

Eventually, though, the tension between contempt from above and popularity from below snapped. He had long predicted his own bloody demise, but his followers assumed it was another metaphor. Soon, though, it was unfolding before their eyes: the culmination of a week which began with huge crowds hailing him as he rode into the capital city on a donkey—a blatant nod towards a famous piece of literature describing a king who would arrive on precisely such an animal. Authorities, already on edge at this perceived threat to their power, found themselves pushed further into a corner when Jesus marched into the temple—the centre of national life—and smashed the place up in protest at the questionable financial practices housed there.

Events spiralled fast. Local leaders manoeuvred the occupying forces into seeking Jesus' arrest, paying off one of his most constant companions to lead them right to him. All his friends scattered. Some lied their way to safety when stopped and questioned—pretended they never knew him. Others simply dropped off the radar altogether. At his sham trial, his release was put to the popular vote, like a macabre ancient spin on *The X Factor*, and the populace opted for a murderous local insurrectionist to be freed in preference to Jesus. Shortly afterwards, he was stripped naked and publicly pinned onto some wooden beams, where he was held in place by shards of metal driven through wrists and feet, as he gasped and gurgled his final breaths. Abandoned and betrayed by friends, crushed by the government, and smeared by his enemies.

Embedded in the Ordinary

Our world is the setting of Jesus' story. He, the main character, is a physical person, raised in a family, subject to betrayal and vulnerable to physical harm. The setting—Roman-occupied Palestine—is historically distinct. His words are recorded in both the common regional language of Greek and his local tongue of Aramaic, and he spoke them while wearing a robe like his contemporaries, participating in the local economy, and becoming subject to shame and condemnation for his choice of companions. Echoed in his narrative are the themes of our lives—friendship, family tensions, work, storytelling—and the kinds of events we see every day in the news: massacre, political and religious corruption, and nationalism.

If Jesus shows us God, then the picture he provides is one which—for all its remarkable features—is strikingly embedded in the ordinary. We encounter no fantastic distant plains. Winged horses and serpent-haired nemeses are entirely absent. Only events unfolding *at this time* and *in that place*: a God embracing human history and those of us who live it.

As such, it runs counter to many of our intuitions about the world and our place in it. The poet Stephen Crane, for example, writes:

A man said to the universe:

"Sir, I exist!"

"However," replied the universe,

"The fact has not created in me

A sense of obligation."[37]

Human existence, for Crane, unfolds against the backdrop of a coldly indifferent cosmos. The journalist Christopher Hitchens, shortly before his death from cancer, echoed Crane by describing himself as one born into a universe which "doesn't know I'm here and won't notice when I'm gone."[38] Likewise Calvin, the comic-strip character who wanders through life with his tiger friend Hobbes, bellows at the stars, "I'm significant", only to then mutter to himself, "Screamed the dust speck".[39] Crane, Hitchens, Calvin and many others assume that reality is essentially impersonal and God— by implication—is either absent or disinterested.

Rubbing against the grain of such perceptions is the story of Jesus. It describes not the universe but the one who sourced all reality as anything but indifferent. Jesus is warmly drawn to people. They may be specks, but he himself has willingly become one too. He treats others with an affection out of all proportion to their physical size. He behaves as though he *does* have a sense of obligation. The scream that we are significant emanates not from us but from deep within him. *I will embrace this world,* the story seems to have him say, *even if it kills me.* God, in Jesus, is pictured moving *towards* us.

We humans, in the story, are also reframed. But not as courageous seekers of the truth: spiritual Indiana Joneses daringly uncovering an inert God hidden in some obscure cobwebbed corner of our world. Instead, we are more like Bilbo Baggins at the start of *The Hobbit,* happily puffing on his pipe in the sunlit, verdant Shire, when the wizard Gandalf approaches and announces, "I am looking for someone to share in an adventure": an unsolicited invitation which redirects the course of Bilbo's morning and, indeed, his life.[40] The dynamic is one of God coming to us. "You could have taken your hand and rubbed it across the rough wood of the cross of Jesus," someone once wrote, and you would have "gotten a splinter" in it, so near did he approach.[41]

Experience Reclassified

If, in Jesus, we catch a glimpse of God—not simply of how he *was* but of his character and nature *right now*—then our own sense of "something more" can be read not as simply our glitching imaginations, nor as an accidental brushing-up against the transcendent, but as something much more intentional. John, one of the first writers to explore how Jesus might show us God, describes him as "the true light that gives light to everyone ... coming into the world".[42] For John, God is actively shedding "light" on everyone; reality, he implies, is suffused with a subtle undercurrent of divine invitation. We sense that there is something more because, as someone once described it to me, "God is flirting with us".[43] It's not just that God *did* reach out to humanity in Jesus. It's that he, the Jesus-shaped God, continues to do so even now.

In the process we undergo a reclassification. We are lifted from the shelf labelled "seekers of God" and moved to one marked "sought by God". We are the objects of his interest. Similarly, our sense of the transcendent, those little hints we find all around us, change from *incidental* to *possibly intentional*, perhaps even *invitational*. Those occasions when we have had a sense that maybe there is something more become— when read through the lens of Jesus' life—the possible approach of God.

If God, in Jesus, embedded himself in a tangible human life, inhaling air through physical lungs, stepping in places we can still visit today, perhaps he has also given you a sense of himself through the concrete physical realities of your existence—the art which inspires you, the music that moves you, the stars which fill you with wonder, and the people who populate your life. Perhaps, as the poet Tennyson wrote, "Closer is He than breathing, and nearer than hands and feet"[44]— infusing our material world with his presence.

Maybe, even in these moments, as your eyes scan these paragraphs, God is neither indifferent nor uninterested. If he is like Jesus, then his receptivity to you is not grounded in any qualities you possess or lack. He cannot be dissuaded by others from associating with you. You could be the most moral person on earth or the sketchiest oddball in your town—it would make no difference; you would still be one to whom he would murmur, *I am looking for someone to share in an adventure*, endowing you with a significance beyond your speck-like proportions. *Sir*, you might say, *I exist*. To which not the universe but the one without whom there would be no cosmos would reply, *And I have taken upon myself a sense of obligation*.

Few people who claim to have experienced the transcendent speak of having "found God". They instead tend to describe God as having approached them. "Found when I wasn't looking, heard when I wasn't listening," is how one poet summarises it.[45] "I once was lost," goes the classic hymn "Amazing Grace", "but now am *found*".[46] God, these writers insist, took a step towards them before they ever glanced back in response. Maybe we, too, are seen when we aren't looking and heard when we aren't listening, and our urge to tilt our heads towards him issues from his nearness to us.

What we mean when we say, "God" will profoundly shape our level of interest in considering him further. Perhaps God, if he exists, is not like Jesus. Maybe we do indeed live in a cold, impersonal reality, and our desire for something more is a cruel joke played on us by our own brains. Perhaps, at best, we are observed by a distant, unmoved spiritual energy.

Yet, even as we consider this possibility, the intriguing prospect remains that God does not simply exist but that he has a trajectory and it is towards us.

>Pause and Consider (or Discuss)

1. How does the story of Jesus compare with how you typically imagine God? Where are the overlaps and the contrasts?

2. Have you ever considered that your sense of something more may be invitational and not only accidental—that God may be reaching out to you? How might your past experiences be reframed if viewed from this perspective?

3. If God were "neither indifferent nor uninterested", then what would you want to say to him?

Chapter Five

Messy and
> Complicated

Jesus divided opinion. Even the high point of his popularity—a slow ride through streets lined with adoring faces, each person jostling for a clearer view, many of them screaming adulation in his direction—turned out simply to be the set-up for the punchline, five days later, of his brutal public murder.[47] All signs of his fans dissipated and in their place was a mob straining their vocal cords to screech, "Crucify him": a desperate collective plea to nail the man to some timber and watch him squirm in pain until they were rid of him once and for all.[48]

As at the end, so at the beginning. His first recorded public speech also provoked two very different reactions from those present.[49] One account of it describes many people who "spoke well of him and were amazed".[50] Almost immediately afterwards, though, we read of a rabble so "furious" at his words that "they got up, drove him out of the town, and took him to the brow of the hill on which the town was built, in order to throw him off the cliff".[51] Jesus, it seems, could consistently provoke those around him to either intense loyalty or homicidal reflexes, all within the briefest span of time.

In vivid and bloody strokes, the story of Jesus sketches the range of reactions we can have to the possibility of God. Some find the prospect intriguing, even attractive. When British actor Phil Daniels, famed from the television soap opera *EastEnders* and various cult films, was asked by *The Guardian* newspaper to name his greatest fear, he replied very succinctly: what haunted him most, he said, was the possibility "that I, as an atheist, am right".[52] The idea of God may not be one he affirms, but its appeal endures, and—like a wistful onlooker lingering at the back of the crowd—he finds himself still throwing furtive glances in the direction of the transcendent each time an inkling of it brushes past.

Philosopher Thomas Nagel, also a self-described atheist, has a very different perspective. In one of the most revealing and vulnerable passages of his work, he admits:

> "I want atheism to be true and am made uneasy by the fact that some of the most intelligent and well-informed people I know are religious believers. It isn't just that I don't believe in God and, naturally, hope that I'm right in my belief. It's that I hope there is no God! I don't want there to be a God; I don't want the universe to be like that."[53]

Nagel, in contrast to Daniels, appears to describe himself as one reaching around for the nearest available knife, ready to slide its blade between the divine ribs should opportunity arise—more likely to tip him off a precipice than applaud in wonder.

Nagel and Daniels seem, at first glance, to be perched at distant ends of a spectrum. Let's coin it the Nagel-Daniels Scale:

Nagel	Daniels
I wish God were not real	**I wish God were real**

Frequently, when speaking with audiences about the themes of this book, I will ask participants where they would pin *their* names on this scale. Are they, like Nagel, also discomforted, even antagonistic, when the subject of God arises? Or, perhaps, do they identify more with the "I hope this is real" sentiments of Phil Daniels? Maybe they sit nestled somewhere in between the two extremes: possibly in the middle or slightly inclining towards one end?

Animated and thoughtful discussion usually hums through the room as everyone seeks to identify their own stance. You, too, may have some instinctive sense of how you would respond and where your fingertip would fall on the line. Curiously, though, swift and definite conclusions are often elusive. It seems, from the many conversations I've had on this topic, that many of us are not at either extreme, nor even suspended halfway, but simultaneously at both ends: drawn and repelled, intrigued and unsettled, open and closed, all at the same time.

This is as true for fervent believers as for convinced atheists. Francis Thompson, a poet in the Roman Catholic tradition, described himself as one constantly darting for cover from a God he pictures as an unrelenting canine sniffing at his trail. His best-known poem begins:

I fled Him, down the nights and down the days;

I fled Him, down the arches of the years;

I fled Him, down the labyrinthine ways

Of my own mind; and in the mist of tears

I hid from Him.[54]

Striking lines from a self-identified believer. God, it transpires, is a complicated and messy subject for any of us. Indifference, undoubtedly, can be one response. But so too can oscillating between a whole range of other points on the continuum.

All of which echoes a plot twist in the stories of Jesus. It turns out, if you read the tale of his final week attentively, that the crowds of Nagels calling for his execution and the sea of Daniels intrigued by his presence were not two opposing factions. Instead they were indistinguishable citizens of the same city. Those hands which applauded his first public speech were, likewise, the very ones which moments later shoved him towards the ledge. Jesus divided opinion, not only between people but also within them. Perhaps he specifically, or God in general, has a similar effect on you.

The Elusiveness of Neutrality

God is tricky, in part, because we cannot contemplate him with cool detachment. It's not like assessing (say) the existence of a rare bird such as the scarlet-banded barbet, with all we require being a careful reading of appropriate sources, along with the input of ornithologically inclined friends. Nor does God resemble a snippet of unfamiliar music that we catch unexpectedly on our streaming service or radio, only for us to either skip to another station or artist, or add it to our favourites. Detachment is more elusive when it comes to the question of God.

To say "God" is to reference the one on whom all things are contingent and the source of the reality whose corridors we pace. We all, to borrow the imagery of chapter 2, inhabit the circle of this universe. And, therefore, to affirm it as rooted in an other—even belonging to that other—is also to make a similar statement about ourselves; we too may belong to, or be rooted in, someone other than ourselves.

Perhaps we could remain distant from the matter if all we admitted were the bare possibility of the cosmos having a personal source, which we might, for purposes of convenience, allow ourselves to label "God". But once we slide towards the imagery of God suggested by Jesus—approaching us, seeing us when we weren't looking, hearing us when we weren't listening, calling us to share in an adventure—neutrality begins to strain.

It's not just the obvious and legitimate stuff which unsettles us, like the abuses of religion or the obnoxiousness of many religious people—all our worst stereotypes of unhinged God-botherers bursting in on our imagination in one repulsive hoard. Our unease lies much deeper than these exterior factors. Even when we sweep all the unpleasant imagery from our minds, still we remain disquieted by the possibility of a God who is real and interested in us, possessing a will and desire independent of our own. We, like Phil Daniels, are drawn, and, like Thomas Nagel, we recoil.

Reflecting on my own mixed feelings towards God, I've come to see them as rooted in several locations. One is summed up neatly in an old science-fiction paperback I once plucked from the dusty lower shelf of an antique bookshop. Part of a trilogy by Chronicles of Narnia author C.S. Lewis, it opens with a man walking across an empty field at dusk, en route to the house of an old friend: a professor recently returned from a pioneering space exploration. This academic has brought with him, stored in otherworldly containers, some strange luminous creatures unlike anything ever seen on Earth.

Each onward step the protagonist takes heightens his own fear. He worries that his host has been naive. That he has invited a malevolent and destructive force into his own home. Even facilitated an interplanetary invasion. How little we know of other worlds and how, he wonders, can we trust something so different to ourselves? As darkness falls and fog encroaches, he steps off the road onto a pathway beside the silhouettes of an abandoned industrial complex and finds that another terror has seeped in. He, the narrator, writes that the cause of this fresh horror crystallises when he finally arrives at the darkened windows of his destination, eases the door open, and catches his first glimpse of the new arrivals:

"My fear was now of another kind. I felt sure that the creature was what we call 'good', but I wasn't sure whether I liked 'goodness' so much as I had supposed. This is a very terrible experience. As long as what you are afraid of is something evil, you may still hope that the good may come to your rescue. But suppose you struggle through to the good and find that it also is dreadful? How if food itself turns out to be the very thing you can't eat, and home the very place you can't live, and your very comforter the person who makes you uncomfortable? Then, indeed, there is no rescue possible: the last card has been played."[55]

Lewis, who often wove observations on God into his novels, precisely describes the unease I have with the possibility of a God for whom my whole being is an open book: one whose unwavering gaze encompasses all I am or have thought or felt—what I have done, yes, and also what has been done to me. I am naked and seen in my entirety. Exposed before a goodness and light I cannot conquer.

My discomfort is further heightened because the light is conscious: self-aware, choosing, discerning, communicating. If God is so personal that he can be fully manifested by a human being—Jesus—then I am not confronting a system I can game, nor a cosmic mechanism I can master. I am dealing with personhood and will. This means that I can't simply do the right things, be they moral or religious, and then lapse into self-congratulation. A personal God calls me towards interpersonal connection.

Engagement with God, though, can never be a meeting of equals. It is a mismatch—he possessing the unconquerable quality Lewis describes in his novel, while I am but another element in the universe of which he is the source. God, in Jesus, is shown to be both ghostable and even killable: willing to be violently rejected by those who owe their very existence to him. But he is never portrayed as controllable. Jesus himself summarised his critics' complaints towards him as "We played the flute for you, and you did not dance; we sang a dirge, and you did not mourn".[56] His moves were always awkwardly beyond their choreography.

Such an untameable God is a threat to my own autonomy. Once, when walking along an empty street at night, trying to pray, my mind wandered towards an exercise in imagination: picturing what I would do if I met Jesus around the next corner. Part of me felt I might walk towards him and embrace him warmly. Yet, almost concurrently, I also saw myself punching him in the face. Because I didn't want him wrecking my plans and taking over my life and stirring everything up so it all became uncomfortable. C.S. Lewis could be writing of my feelings towards God when he has his narrator muse:

> "Here at last was a bit of that world from beyond the
> world, which I had always supposed that I loved and

*desired, breaking through and appearing to my senses:
and I didn't like it, I wanted it to go away. I wanted
every possible distance, gulf, curtain, blanket, and
barrier to be placed between it and me."* [57]

These, then, are a few fragments of my own discomfort
towards God. They are several of the reasons why I see
something of Thomas Nagel in me, even at the very
moments when my interest in God is most piqued.
You may have your own motives for hesitation—fear
of what God might have you become, disappointment
from past moments when you *did* ask something of him
and it didn't materialise, or simple unease at shifting
your position on something so significant. God remains
tricky for each of us in different ways.

Honest Starting Points

The poet W.H. Auden once described his craft as "the
clear expression of mixed feelings".[58] And few subjects
more swiftly reveal our inner poet than that of God.
Discussion of him brings into focus an assortment of
reactions and impulses. Curiosity is provoked. Even
attraction. So too may be distaste, indifference and
hostility. We find ourselves to be spiritual seekers and,
even in the same moment, spiritual evaders. Divided
within ourselves between openness and hesitation.

Identifying the causes of this complexity, though,
may be less useful than simply acknowledging it. Tomáš
Halík points out that discussions of God too frequently
begin with a debate over whether or not he exists. Halík,
a renowned philosopher and theologian, doesn't deny
that this is a vital and fascinating topic. But it is not, he

suggests, the optimum starting point. Instead, he says, it is more helpful to begin not with "Does God exist?" but "Do I *want* him to exist?"[59] No honest engagement with God can occur without a sincere response to this question, even if the answer is just "Sometimes", "A bit", or "Not really".

Such an admission does nothing to deter God. Not, at least, if Jesus is our measure of his character. He was described by one contemporary as "knowing the thoughts of [others'] hearts", yet he consistently moved towards them.[60] He did so in each of the stories which opened this chapter—deciding to give a speech to an audience who would attempt to murder him before he finished, and mapping out a journey towards the very city where he would be tortured to death. God may divide opinion, even within me, but it seems that we do no such thing for him—he sees us as we are, and his trajectory remains towards us.

>Pause and Consider (or Discuss)

1. Where would you place yourself on the Nagel-Daniels scale? What do you think pulls you towards the Daniels end and what towards the Nagel end?

2. What most resonated with you in this chapter's description of the author's own discomfort with the possibility of God? What might you have added or changed had you written this section?

3. Why do you think we sometimes find it hard to think of ourselves not only as spiritual seekers, but also as spiritual evaders? In what ways do you think "spiritual seeking" manifests itself for you? How about "spiritual evasion"?

Chapter Six

Drawing
> Closer

Wooden slats cover the windows. Nobody remembers its last occupants. Once a pub, it sat for decades alone beside a now-abandoned train station. When, in recent years, new houses and streets emerged in the adjoining fields, a lively community taking shape all around, its grimy façade remained unchanged. The surrounding rusting fence, topped with wire barbs, pushed its crumbling brickwork slowly to the periphery of local adults' imaginations, all the while seeding legends and ghostly tales among the village youth.

One day, playing sick from school, you sneak from your house. Through the back fence, to avoid neighbours' prying eyes, and on to the abandoned inn. In your bag is a saw. All the saws, in fact, that you could find. One of them, you hope, will slice through metal. The first one breaks on the gate's padlock, its teeth curling against the thick steel, and you discard it. Then another. Four take damage in their own way. The fifth, though, is much narrower, and you apply it not to the lock but the metallic fence post, and here it begins to carve the slightest of lines, which grows to a groove, and your hopes rise as it works a third of the way through, halfway, two thirds. Until...

It snaps. Not the upright, as you had hoped, but the blade. Thwarted but undeterred you use both palms to make the final push against it, applying the force of your arms, then your back, and finally your legs, which can gain no purchase against the sticky mud beneath your feet. Then you kick. A vague imitation of martial-arts moves once seen on television. Again and again your sole pounds the pole until it begins to first incline away from you, and then eventually bend at a right angle, causing the wire around to flop downwards. Treading it to the ground, you march across it, pausing only momentarily when the sharpened edge of the newly-severed post gashes through your trousers and skin. A glance at your bloodied calf suggests it's only a flesh wound, and you continue across the barren ground to the nearest window.

Its wooden slats are easily prised away with the claw of your hammer, and you are able to clamber through the opened frame, again slicing your thumb on a remaining shard of glass. You leap down onto the pub floor, and gaze across the room—lit only by a shaft of light in which dance a congested swarm of dust particles—and towards the object of your quest. Beneath a discoloured cream sheet in the opposite corner lies an item of legend: a pinball machine, once famed among a generation—those who topped its maximum score of 999,999 would receive a code which, the makers promised, could be exchanged for 30 one-kilogram bars of pure gold. The offer, your research suggests, remains valid, though all machines were assumed destroyed. Except one. Its whereabouts, until now, long forgotten.

Casting the cover aside, you behold it for a moment, and then crouch to connect its plug to the mains. Incredibly, all these years later, the current remains active, and the machine jolts to life in a burst of neon and a cascade of electronic sound effects. So it begins. Five hours you stay that first day. Sweat soaking your clothes as you smash the buttons almost without pause. Mostly, it seems, your moves are rooted in frustration—none of the online simulations had prepared you for the subtleties and quirks of the physical original. You limp home that afternoon, carefully replacing the slats and re-erecting the fence, and spend the remaining hours of the day hunched over a computer, searching for information to help better your paltry high score of 42,176.

The next day, you shower, briefly—the wounds on your leg and hand now encrusted—and repeat the previous day's journey. Another five hours, and you attain 55,298. The following morning, shivering with the slightest of fevers, you return and break 75,000 for the first time. The temperature becomes a fixture— almost welcome as you no longer need to fake illness to your parents—and by the end of the week you have managed 210,371. It takes several more days and tens of hours to arrive at 832,694. By this time you wince each time your foot presses on the floor. Showers have become sporadic, and when you next have one, you see the line of discoloured inflammation bubbling along your calf. "Are you sure you don't need to see a doctor?" your mother asks, but you wave her away.

Week 3 begins promisingly. 932,987. By now it is harder to remain upright, and you perch atop a bar stool, hunched forward in complete absorption, and by Tuesday you're at 981,006. Your pockets are stuffed with pills intended to stave off the shivering. Pus has glued the trouser fabric to your leg now. But you press on. Wednesday brings 997,591. Thursday is similar. And then Friday. Scarcely able to control your shaking hands, you finally, finally, see every figure on the display become a nine: 999,999. Victory. Every light flashes, and each sound rings in celebration. Now the code. You slide from the stool and reach into your pocket for a pen and paper. You note down the first digit, the second. You are about to be a millionaire. It's all going to pay off.

But then a flicker. A glitch. The machine hesitates. Your thoughts freeze, and before you can act, the lights fail, and the smell of burning plastic fills your nostrils. And the code is gone. You punch the machine. Kick it and cause a jolt of sharp pain to run along your leg. But it isn't coming back. It's now only you, in the darkness, your overheated body and festering limb slumped on the ground, consumed by a sense of loss as beside you flames begin to lick around the casing. It's melting, and so are your dreams.

Beyond Pinball

God, it is widely imagined, is something like this mythical pinball machine. Our access and proximity to him, and the vividness of our relationship with him, are assumed to correlate to our personal performance. The capacities we require to know God are rarely understood to be wire-cutting, pinball and housebreaking. They may be morality or goodness. Or perhaps aptitude with religious rituals, texts, vocabulary or spiritual practices. We and our works— our kindness and thoughtfulness, morality and hard effort—are, on this account, what win favour with God. They allow us to first break down the fences and then play the game. And so one who wishes to know God must, it is expected, be a certain kind of person or first become a different kind of person.

We are like Ryan Stone, a fictional NASA astronaut played by Sandra Bullock in the film *Gravity*, who becomes stranded in space and confronted by the fearful possibility of her impending death. As hope fades, her thoughts turn to whether anyone will say a prayer for her when she dies. "I'd say one for myself, but I've never prayed in my life before," she says, amid tears. "Nobody ever taught me how; nobody ever taught me how."[61] For Ryan Stone, it is as if there is one group of people who've mastered the skills, rituals and practices of accessing whatever is out there—the housebreakers and pinball whizzes of the transcendent, who understand prayer and all the rest of it. Religious people. Spiritual people. Other people.

If this is true, and expertise and effort really are the key to encountering God, or to him becoming something more than fluttering wings at the periphery of our vision, then we can tumble in one of two directions in response. We might, for example, lapse into despair. Who, if honest about the messy and complicated nature of their attitude to God—the indifference and even hostility explored in the previous chapter—can really be confident about a system where you must win through your own skill and consistency? And if how we lived and treated others were *also* among the criteria for mastering the "game", then, well, maybe we rank in the top half: possibly even with a proverbial score of (say) over 650,000 (which, let's be honest, is much better than some people we could mention). But are any of us attaining 999,999? Possibly somebody somewhere. But it's not me, and I'd hazard a guess it's not you.

Despair, though, is not the only available option. Some skew in another direction: towards cockiness. A swagger in the step and a condescending look towards the rest of us. "Good," they nod as smugness fixes on their lips, "I'd hoped it would be about performance because I am at the top of my game, and if I'm not, then I can always learn to be if I apply my mind to it; all you need is a little self-discipline". Distant from them is the mentality of Aleksandr Solzhenitsyn, a political prisoner in Soviet-era Russia, who wrote following his incarceration:

> "The line separating good and evil passes ... right through every human heart—and through all human hearts. This line shifts. Inside us, it oscillates with the years. And even within hearts overwhelmed by evil, one small bridgehead of good is retained. And even in the best of all hearts, there remains ... an unuprooted small corner of evil."[62]

Solzhenitsyn, renowned as a fiery opponent of abusive governments and systems, isn't advocating a moral relativism which shrugs its shoulders at wrongdoing or pretends that all humans are equally flawed. He is, instead, arguing that anyone who doesn't acknowledge that they too are a mixture of darkness and light, or whose hopes hinge on their own flawless performance, misperceives themselves.

He's issuing a call to realism. "We're so accustomed to disguising ourselves to others," muses a character in the film *The Goldfinch*, "that in the end we become disguised to ourselves".[63] It's no wonder we cheer when the smug inevitably fall; the lie undergirding their cockiness has been exposed, and they've been tugged brutally back to reality, discovering in the process that they are as messy and complicated as everyone else. Perhaps nowhere is such self-righteousness uglier than when couched in God language, and we would be well advised to avoid joining the ranks of the spiritually self-satisfied, boasting of our high scores to ourselves and others.

Both cockiness and despair, though, are misplaced attitudes towards God. If he is like Jesus, then neither effort nor skill are key to encountering him. Picture Jesus at his most famous moment, and you see the battered corpse of a human: beaten, tortured and pinned to beams of wood in the open air. This God, as explored in the third chapter, shows himself to us as a person. And people cannot be played or mastered or won like electronic games. If they can, then we call that "manipulation", and it's safe to say that successfully manipulating God is beyond our capacities. A good

God will, of course, prefer moral actions to immoral ones, kindness to cruelty, and generosity to selfishness. But no friendship, human or divine, can be built only on moral excellence and religious aptitude. When two people wish to draw close to one another, it requires something else altogether.

Coming Together

Picture Jesus' bleeding body again. Not many minutes of life remaining. Jagged shards of metal cutting into his wrists and ankles. Unexpectedly, amid his agonised cries and groans, he exclaims a prayer—"Father, forgive them".[64] It is far from the first time he has spoken of forgiveness, but it is perhaps the most striking; Jesus, when faced with people so antagonistic to him that they would have him die in excruciation, reaches not for vengeance but forgiveness. All he could hold against them he releases.

When people come together and one of them has been indifferent or hostile, it requires forgiveness. To forgive is not to endorse what another has done. Neither is it to minimise the problem and wave it away with a declaration that "It's no big deal" or "I know you had some good reasons for what you did" or to recategorise what has occurred as a mistake or misunderstanding.[65] To forgive is to take a look at the whole ugly mess between the two of you and to determine that it will no longer play any part in how you treat the other. It is the renunciation of the right to retribution rather than a denial that the right exists, and it clears the path to reconciliation.

Forgiveness is simple and straightforward until you

have something to forgive which is neither minor nor imagined. Then it wrenches your gut. It tears you apart to even release your grip slightly on your very legitimate opposition to the perpetrator. You have been wronged, and nothing can ever undo what has occurred. You can't just shrug at injustice or brush it all off casually. When people say, "Why don't you just forgive them?" you know that to do so will wound you deeply, even if it might also release you. Japanese author Kazoh Kitamori describes pain as an inevitable component of embracing those alienated from us—it costs us to remove the obstacle from between us.[66]

It costs Anne Warren, a character in the miniseries *Time*, who loses her husband, Bob, to a drunk driver.[67] He could have been saved, but the culprit, Mark, flees the scene, leaving him to die alone. At the trial she tells Mark that Bob "was twice the man that you are"—a line which eats away at him throughout his years of incarceration for manslaughter. So troubled is Mark that he plans to write a letter to Anne from prison. The letter never reaches her, though, as she refuses all correspondence from her husband's killer.

Mark is eventually released, a humbled and penitent man, and a year later a meeting is arranged with Anne in a café on Southport Pier. Anne enters rigid with caution and refuses Mark's offer of a drink but does slowly sit down. As their conversation proceeds, Anne can barely make eye contact, and when she says she's heard about his letter, he slides it across the table—a single sheet of paper with the word "sorry" written repeatedly from top to bottom.

Between silence and sighs she turns the paper over, etches her address, and says, "If you do write again, I'll read it". As Mark stares in disbelief, Anne continues, "I want to forgive you, you see. I need to forgive you, but I can't. I've tried, and I can't." Then she breathes deeply, restraining her tears, before adding, "But I'll keep on trying; I promise you I'll keep on trying. Maybe one day." It's a hauntingly truthful scene, powerfully reminding viewers that while forgiveness can help set one free, it is never cheap or painless to the one who forgives.

Envisage again Jesus' torn, bleeding form, bruised and teetering on the edge of extinction. Here is a God who looks at his world—every misdeed, both towards him and others—and makes the arduous choice to forgive. "This is my body," he said the night before he died, "given for you".[68] To look on the smashed body of Jesus is to glimpse what occurs when forgiveness is extended for all that will ever need forgiving. It fractures and snaps even God himself.

And it is Jesus broken. Not us. There isn't a skill or effort asked of us to attain forgiveness. Jesus, shortly before his death, borrowed language from the slave market—potent imagery of a local location where those on display had no freedom or agency—and said that he had come to "give his life as a ransom for many": a "ransom" being the price paid for the freedom of a slave.[69] He wasn't urging people to earn their own forgiveness or engineer their own reconciliation with God. Jesus would be the ransom. He is the one who removes the fences, levers away the wooden slats, and smashes the window panes, taking the injuries and pain which come about in the process. He bears the weight of reconciliation on his own shoulders so that our evasion, hostility, and all the accumulated grime of the years no longer need come between us and God.

If Jesus shows us God, then our flair for playing the system—be it moral or religious—will not define our ability to know God. Nor will our high score; and we all have a system for ranking ourselves against others. God is not a mechanism we can master or manipulate nor a hidden object we must recover through great exertions, provoking in us either cockiness or despair. He instead comes to us as a person, Jesus, and demands not that we be broken for anything in our lives but, rather, announces his intention to break himself, enabling us to experience forgiveness and the possibility of reconciliation with him.

>Pause and Consider (or Discuss):

1. Have you ever had the impression that connection with God hinges on our hard work or goodness? If so, who or what do you think helped create that sense?

2. If your relationship with God was dependent on your skill or effort, do you think you would incline more towards cockiness or despair? Or both? Why do you think that is?

3. If God welcomed you based on his own self-breaking forgiveness, rather than the excellence of your performance—"extending forgiveness for all that will ever need forgiving"—in what ways would that be liberating for you, and in what ways might it be unsettling?

Chapter Seven

A Different Kind of > Connection

God invites a response from us. Sometimes it comes almost involuntarily. My dad unexpectedly decided to pray as he bobbed on the surface of the South Pacific Ocean. Prior to that fishing trip, he had been an agnostic: open to the possibility of God's existence but doubtful that the source of our universe would have any interest in him personally. He'd read the stories of Jesus' life and appreciated them for their cultural significance. But he wasn't convinced. God, he had concluded, was not for him.

Metres from the hull of his upturned boat, from which he was desperately attempting to disentangle the cords of his lifejacket following its unexpected capsizing, a menacing grey curve glided silently through the waves. Beside it several more fins moved rapidly. Sharks, in waters known to host great whites, were intently circling. It was at this moment that my father rapidly reassessed his stance towards God. It made sense, in such a setting, to at least attempt a prayer.

Over the following few minutes, he outlined his immediate needs, which included returning home to his pregnant wife. He also made a number of promises and resolutions. Sincere, simple words spoken under great stress, with no pretence of being a great believer. Then he waited. Each passing moment ground away at his hope until, when he was exhausted and desperate, a small fishing vessel floated into view, tacked starboard and welcomed him aboard, instantly removing him from the day's menu.[70]

Dad didn't revise his entire position on God following this incident. He followed through on commitments made and was inclined towards the possibility that his rescue had been an answer to prayer. But he continued to leave life with God to other people. It was enough for him to return safely home for the birth of my sister and for the whole experience to fade into the past.

Similar urgent prayers, often only whispered or thought, spring from most of us at some point. Job interviews, first dates, coursework deadlines and exams, or medical procedures and diagnoses—it doesn't usually take a shark attack for us to ask God to enter a moment or situation. Sometimes it even feels as though our pleas are heeded.

Forgiveness, explored in the previous chapter, sometimes appears on our cosmic shopping lists. We might ask for it after, or even during, actions and attitudes we know to be less than ideal. Believing that

God forgives is comforting in these situations. Knowing it means so much to him that he broke himself to achieve it only cements our confidence that he would grant forgiveness when requested. Yet, to view forgiveness in this way—as something we can order, pocket and walk away with—is to misunderstand its purpose.

Forgiveness is never simply *for* another person. It is something which occurs *between* them. It is not an ends but a means: a way for two people to be reconciled. Forgiveness is central to the story of Jesus not because he thought it would be a pleasant object for people to enjoy on their own—like a child absorbed in a Rubik's cube—but because he is inviting us towards a connection more profound than occasional rescues from sharks, illness and bad dates.

Modes of Connection

A London basement was where I first vividly grasped what God was inviting us towards. Over the preceding year, I had become intrigued by the possibility of a different way of relating to God. Books of personal stories began lining my shelves. A short autobiography, penned by a former gang leader, told of a broken man—son of an abusive mother—pulled from his life of violence and transformed into a person of peace after his encounter with a follower of Jesus.[71] The memoir of a politician, a man who became mired in corruption, described how he chose to plead guilty because God had helped him love truth more than lies.[72]

These dramatic tales, though, were less compelling than the everyday ones. I sourced the biography of the individual who first befriended the gang leader and was warmed by his sheer ordinariness.[73] God at work in the life of a desperate criminal was one thing. His nearness to a nervous family man was another. Much later I would be absorbed by the autobiography of musician Johnny Cash, whose account intertwined devotion to God with bizarre incidents such as embroiling himself in a fight with an ostrich and subsequently developing an addiction to painkillers.[74] It was oddly compelling to read of God at work in the mess and randomness.

When I arrived in the London cellar, these descriptions of God began bleeding off the page and into my surroundings. I was in the city for a month to gain experience in several faith-based community projects. My host, an extroverted Zimbabwean named Joseph, given to loudly praying in his car, had dragged me along to various gatherings—this one a dawn event arranged by a local church and attended by maybe 50 people.[75] He had peeled away to catch up with someone when I found myself alone—tea mug in one hand, Danish pastry in the other—with two conversation partners, both dressed for the office, ready to clock-in at a nearby business.[76]

They were discussing God in concrete terms. Each was sharing what he had been doing in their lives during the previous week: things he'd impressed on them, ways he'd shaped their approach to difficult situations at work, and their sense that he'd been with them as they navigated awkward relationships. The whole exchange was entirely unaffected. They spoke of God as naturally as I might describe buying a baguette or recall key moments from a football match. God, I swiftly apprehended, was not a theory or concept to them—they, like my host, Joseph, and like bird-wrestling pill-popper Johnny Cash, viewed him as real and active in their lives.

Years later I would compare what I had observed to the trajectory of my son's relationship with Gheorghe Hagi, the legendary former Barcelona and Real Madrid midfielder. Jackson was six when I first showed him old footage of Hagi making pinpoint passes or skipping past defenders to dispatch the ball into the top corner of the net. As Jackson gazed on the grainy images, recorded on flickering videotape, something shifted; he had moved from ignorance to knowledge.

Another three years passed before they met in person. Jackson, playing for a youth team aligned with a larger professional club, was selected to walk onto the pitch with the senior players before the game. In the tunnel, as he waited to enter, Jackson glimpsed the opposing team's manager and instantly recognised the face—Gheorghe Hagi. He walked over and initiated a very short conversation. Their brief exchange of words transitioned Hagi from being an object of Jackson's awareness to one with whom he had communicated.

What didn't happen next, sadly, was for Hagi to become a close family friend—one who came and ate meals at our house or took my boys to the park for personal training sessions or who spent hours in our living room as we enjoyed one another's company. Had that occurred, though, it would have further developed their connection from simple interaction to personal involvement. Jackson would have journeyed from ignorance to knowledge, then to contact, and finally to friendship.

In London, as I sipped my tea and listened, I was struck by the fact that the office workers beside me seemed to be at this third stage of interpersonal connection. It wasn't simply that they were aware of some facts about Jesus, like a child watching recordings of a retired footballer. Nor was it that they sometimes made contact by praying in difficult circumstances, resembling Jackson striking up a pre-match chat or my father crying out for deliverance from sharks. Instead, God had become woven into the mundanities of their everyday experience.

This weaving into the ordinary echoes the stories of Jesus. He appears, when you read them, to spend his days in unspectacular places. One ancient biography introduces him walking by a river, before hosting people in his accommodation, sipping wine at a wedding, conversing in the evening cool, catching his breath by a well, pausing at a site hosting local disabled people, serving food on a hillside, meandering across a lake in a boat, visiting a friend's grave, attending a national festival and eating a meal in a house.[77] He does also enter *some* religious sites, such as synagogues and a temple, but he is far from restricted to them—his footprints land everywhere.

His encounters in these locations are with a recognisable range of characters: local tradesmen, an influential teacher wrestling with his own beliefs, a woman with a complicated marital history, another woman subject to abuse from neighbours, a man struggling with incurable illness, a civil servant caring for his sick child, a son reduced to begging on the streets and disowned by his family, two sisters wrapped in grief, and the list continues.[78] Not once, in all these interactions, does he have duplicate conversations. His character remains steady and consistent, but he meets people in their unique locations and addresses them within their specific circumstances.

This small London gathering was another track from the same playlist—nobody there had identical narratives, but each could speak tangibly of God's involvement in their ordinary places of work, rest and residence. And not without humour: I couldn't burst their bubbles of pomposity or doubtlessness because they had none. Even frustration with God was aired as readily as thankfulness. If God's forgiveness was aimed at reconciliation, then here, I concluded, were people experiencing it. "These people," I commented to a friend that evening, "they have something I don't".

Origin Stories

In the books I had read and in the conversations around London—both over breakfast and with Joseph—each individual could map a shift in their relationship with God. Some had experienced an intense moment of transition so distinct that they could almost name the minute and hour. Others had a fuzzy period, over the course of months or even longer, of sliding, almost imperceptibly, towards a different place.

Nobody saw themselves as the initiators of this change. God is at work around all of us, whether we perceive it or not, and if he is Jesus-shaped, then he is reaching out to us, both through the stories of Jesus and also through our sense of something more. To be alive is to experience God, and he whispers to us in everything. Our renewed connection with him begins, then, not because we find him or conjure him into reality but because we respond affirmatively to his invitation and pause our resistance to him.

This pausing is neither moral reformation nor a proffering of vows regarding future conduct. Johnny Cash, mired in addiction, says things changed when "I asked [God] to go to work on me, then and there": not cleaning up his act before responding but inviting God into the mess.[79] If Jesus has broken himself for our forgiveness, then it would be strange if we, in turn, had to achieve something before responding—as if our bold lifestyle changes could tear open an archway to God. "I am the door," Jesus said of himself, meaning the opening is already there, all barriers between us are removed, and our part is only to take advantage of what has been achieved and walk through.[80]

We do so with our doubts and questions unshelved. My dad, 16 years after his maritime rescue, finally responded to God's invitation, surprising himself and everyone who knew him, and for the last three decades of his life was a follower of Jesus. Not long before he died, we were walking on the chalky downs of Salisbury Plain, near his home, and I made some remark along the lines of "You used to be something of a sceptic, didn't you, Dad?" He paused as he stared out over the vale below and then turned towards me and said, "You know, I'm still a sceptic really, Luke; I'm just a sceptic who believes".[81]

Ironclad certainty, then, is not a prerequisite to knowing God any more than in other interpersonal relationships. Friendships often begin with caution; then confidence grows, and even fluctuates, over the years. "I believe," someone once said to Jesus; "help my unbelief"—a concise model for any of us wanting to respond to him.[82] We don't need complex, eloquent speeches. Our response could be as simple as "Here I am": a way of telling God "I'm no longer resisting; you've found me".[83]

A friend told me that the turning point in his relationship with God came when he made the straightforward statement "You are God, and I am not". Welcoming God, he said, implied aligning ourselves with him—or, at least, what we know of him—rather than expecting him to turbocharge *our* agendas, like an electoral candidate waving a Bible in the hope that it legitimises all they want to do anyway. To pray sincerely is to acknowledge that, while God is the source of the whole universe, he is also *our* source and the one on whom *our* whole existence is contingent. One early follower of Jesus pictured us plucking crowns from our heads and placing them at his feet, as if to signify that we and all we curate are ultimately not our own.[84]

God, then, invites a response from us. Not only one of calling for help in difficult moments but also something closer to opening a door and saying, "Come in—you are welcome to be God not only of all reality but also of me". And then, his forgiveness having made possible our reconciliation, something fresh begins seeping into our everyday. "Here a new story begins," writes novelist Fyodor Dostoyevsky, "the story of a person's gradual renewal and gradual rebirth, of their gradual crossing from one world to another, of their acquaintance with a new, as yet unknown reality".[85]

>Pause and Consider (or Discuss)

1. Where would you say you are in terms of the three modes of relationship with God described in the analogy of Jackson's relationship with Hagi—awareness, contact or friendship? Why would you place yourself there?

2. Have you ever considered responding to God's invitation in the way described in the final section? What pulls you towards doing so, and what makes you hesitate?

3. Have you ever observed people who expect God to "turbocharge their agendas, like an electoral candidate waving a Bible in the hope that it legitimises all they want to do anyway"? In what ways do you think (or worry) that responding to God might call into question your agenda?

Chapter Eight

Life
> Together

It was a quick read. Around a hundred pages (not including the endnotes). And now we are here; the final chapter has arrived. You hadn't been sure what to expect when you started. Title and subject were intriguing enough for you to at least scan the opening paragraphs, and then you kept going, perhaps drawn onwards by the content or simply because this is your habit with short books—see them through to the end. And now, pages from its conclusion, threads still hang loose.

"Everything comes into focus eventually" was the promise of the very first line, and while you know this was partially a reference to the eyesight of newborn babies, that initial segment also closed with a question—"Will everything really come into focus eventually?" God, through the lines of this book, may (perhaps) have begun to make a little more sense, but how will the image become sharper and the experience more real? How, beyond this text, will God become a part of your everyday?

The experience of God has been likened, by Søren Kierkegaard, the Danish philosopher, to someone segueing from examining a music sheet to playing those notes on a physical instrument. "Only in a figurative sense does music exist when it is being read," he says. "It *actually* exists only when it is being performed."[86] To know God, he insists, requires not only adequate theoretical information but an encounter with him, the tones of which reverberate far beyond the page.

I was in a red phone box when the faint background sounds of this possibility became unignorable. It was the day after the breakfast encounter described in the previous chapter, and I was considering curtailing my London visit. There was something both captivating and unsettling in meeting so many people who refused to store God in neat containers labelled "religion" or "theoretical debate" and who seemed content to let him run loose around the place. As I stood there, though, gathering my thoughts in seclusion from the city crowds, a sense of unexpected clarity suddenly pressed in; I needed to stay in the capital. Something, I felt oddly convinced, was stirring.

The following evening, having tentatively decided to remain, I was walking through Leicester Square, past the glowing frontages of picture houses and restaurants. Petrichor, the smell of warm rain on earthy surfaces, filled the air, and the friend I was with—to whom I had earlier commented, "These people have something I don't"—wandered momentarily away, leaving me alone beside some iron railings. Looking up, I noticed a man shuffling slowly towards me from the spot where he had been begging. He didn't ask for money and, in fact, refused my offers. Instead, following a brief conversation, during which I learned he was homeless, he requested a pen and paper, on which he scribbled a biblical reference which, he said, was for me. Then he wandered away into the crowds, leaving me clutching the scrap in my hand.

Some hours later, when my friend and I were able to locate a Bible, we pulled out the folded note, found the reference, and I read it aloud. It was a segment of poetic text, often seen as referring to Jesus, in which God speaks figuratively about dry grass turning green, drought-ridden lands experiencing rainfall, and trees brimming with fruit.[87] It almost perfectly encapsulated the pull we both increasingly felt: a desire for the reality of God to grow and bud in our lives, as it was doing in these others we had met. We each decided right then to ask God to forgive our resistance and prayed together for him to begin in us what we had witnessed in them.

We were we responding to God's invitation. Our experience echoed a tiny poem by the fantasy writer George MacDonald, entitled "The Shortest and Sweetest of Songs", which reads simply:

Come.
Home.[88]

Our response to God was such a homecoming. And yet, like most homecomings, its sweetness was not in the drama of the arrival but the warmth of the place we had entered. Our destination was a God we had both, in our own separate ways, come to understand through the prism of Jesus—a God who had revealed himself as a person and whose trajectory was towards us. One who had given us enough shadow to hide and sufficient light to see, and yet who was undeterred by our indifference or even our hostility. His welcome was predicated on his self-breaking forgiveness and not our own skill or effort.

God, like any good host, did not instantly increase the music of this experience to eardrum-shredding levels. Instead, snippets wove in and out of my days, as if a nearby busker was slowly drifting into earshot. The following week, for example, I went for a long walk and decided to pray—only, I didn't really *pray* in anything like the form I assumed prayer should take. I just spoke to God the things I felt like saying, and then I lapsed into silence. My own words totalled maybe 15 minutes, and yet they entirely reordered my understanding of verbal engagement with God into something involving my ordinary language and thoughts directed towards him in whatever location I happened to be at that moment.

My experience is echoed by that of comedian Frank Skinner, who describes his prayer life as a "dip into a long ongoing conversation with thousands of tabs left open and no helpful 'new readers start here' summaries or simplifications for the neutral observer".[89] We are engaging with the personal God within the complexities and nuances of our own existence. And, like in any conversation, communication flows both ways. Sometimes with his insistent pressing, as in the phone box, and at other times in more overt ways—visions, dreams, even physical experiences.

The Civil Rights activist Martin Luther King Jr., for example, recalled that in one of his lowest moments, following death threats during the early days of the Montgomery bus boycott, he retreated to his kitchen to pray, wondering whether to continue. While there, he recounted, "I could hear an inner voice saying to me, 'Martin Luther, stand up for righteousness. Stand up for justice. Stand up for truth. And lo, I will be with you, even until the end of the world.'"[90] It steeled him afresh, and he would later proclaim:

> "I'll tell you, I've seen the lightning flash.
> I've heard the thunder roll.
> I felt sin-breakers dashing,
> trying to conquer my soul.
> But I heard the voice of Jesus saying
> still to fight on."[91]

In small ways, with individuals around me, or in more expansive ways, his voice has also moved me beyond myself and towards others.

His prompting, though, is often closer to a simple reminder than a startling thunderclap. Maybe to have patience with difficult people or better support my wife. To seek justice or serve those marginalised. Or perhaps a quiet reaffirmation of God's commitment to me—a dragging of what I already know but have forgotten to the forefront of my mind. But not always: a couple of weeks into my homecoming, I was queuing outside the Royal Albert Hall with two new friends I'd met that week, and I felt prompted to leave immediately. Confused, I did so and traipsed away to the Tube. Subsequently I was to discover that I had enabled their first date, leaving them alone for friendship to flourish. It was an evening which was to eventually lead to their marriage.

Most consistently, though, I heard from God in the stories of Jesus. His early followers sometimes called him "the Word".[92] He is, they were saying, the articulation of God's character through a human life— the syllables of the divine breathed toward us. "The Word," his friend John writes, "became flesh and lived among us".[93] It therefore soon became my habit to read, or later listen to, a short passage from one of Jesus' earliest biographies and then to speak to him as if he were the one whose interactions I had just witnessed.[94] I was catching sight of God through these narratives— being shaped as I responded.

At times the experience was quite personal, like a song coming only through my headphones. At others it was closer to performing in an impromptu band, as new friends—also finding their way with God—crossed my path and our soundscapes mingled. Helping me find my rhythm was a weekly gathering in the city to which I moved a couple of months after events in London. It was connected with a local church, and we'd meet in someone's living room, eat food and have an open discussion around the stories of Jesus or other early writings from his followers, throwing our questions at them and asking how they intersect with our lives. Here I found a safe context in which to raise queries and learn from others.

Along with another newcomer to this group, I would regularly walk into our town centre and stop in at a small bookshop, nestled in a glass-roofed Victorian arcade crammed with other independent retailers. It sold books on all things theological. A kindly man with whitening hair who staffed the place became a trusted contact for conversation and reading recommendations—helping me select what was most helpful to my current questions. The volumes he sold, and occasionally even gifted, helped me begin thinking more clearly about God: approaching difficult questions rather than avoiding them and intertwining a growing confidence with an increased generosity towards those with differing convictions.

More had come into focus. But not everything. God shows himself to us in the person of Jesus, and people— as we explored earlier—always extend beyond our field of vision; I *knew* God, yes, and yet I was simultaneously in the process of *getting to know* him better. And I have continued to be so down the years, across my darkest times, like suddenly losing my father or emigrating abroad alone, and my happier ones: marriage, children, professional ventures. Mostly, though, the connection hums quietly throughout my ordinary everyday. God has become home to me, and the dry places are now increasingly green.

Personal and Collective

Nobody has a story like mine. Or like yours. God invites a response from us, and yours is unlikely to include extroverted Zimbabweans, crisis moments in a phone box, handwritten notes from homeless people or visits to friendly, old booksellers. It may not even feature narrow escapes from sharks. God's infinite creativity implies that his relationships with each of us will be as varied as those between humans. Within this variety, though, there will be common themes—distinctive characteristics which recur across narratives of coming home to him.

Our willingness to dance from the general to the particular is one such feature. To allow our sense of something more to move us from broad openness to focused exploration. To follow the specifics where they lead us. With Jesus, this means seeing God in his story: one which contains an intriguing suggestion—that he is not simply a compelling historical figure whose life and teachings signpost us to God but is, instead, to borrow words once spoken to his mother, "God with us".[95] Not only a symbol of the one who invites us home but inseparably identifiable with him.

Nowhere is this identification of Jesus with God seen more vividly than in the aftermath of his execution. Within days of Jesus' brutal public annihilation, reports began spreading of his reappearance, in private residences and also public locations like beaches. One document, written not long after, refers casually, as if to a well-worn fact, to him appearing to "more than five hundred" people, and goes on to identify some of the witnesses by name.[96] Jesus was viewed, from very soon after his passing, not as a deceased teacher but as one who is presently alive. And so to say the name "Jesus" is not to mention the dead but address the living.

People, though, clearly don't rise from the dead. Jesus' contemporaries knew this as well as we do. Death's finality is hardly a recent biological discovery—poets and storytellers down the millennia have grappled with our own inevitable extinction. The story of Jesus' resurrection, though, is not about what ordinarily occurs. It describes no repeatable experiment and requires no revision of our scientific principles.[97] Instead, it is a suggestion that at one point in human history, against the narrative flow of all our lives, God did something remarkable, and even death itself, for a time, began to work backwards.[98] Jesus, in the process, was demonstrated to be unique—the source of all life, inextinguishable even by death itself.

Historical arguments for the resurrection are compelling and repay investigation—some excellent resources are highlighted in the endnotes.[99] History, though, is not the only way we might pursue this. The claim is not simply that Jesus *was* alive at some past date but that he *is* alive and knowable today. Our exploration of him will therefore necessarily involve those around us who claim already to have experienced and perceived him. Luke Timothy Johnson, a leading scholar of the early Jesus movement, notes that—alongside the eyewitness testimony and historical indicators—something else amplified the early Christians' conviction that Jesus was a present reality. In their earliest writings, they describe the experience of his "presence and power" not simply "as discrete events in the past, but as the condition of their continued existence".[100] They were, in other words, participants in communities that perceived the living Jesus as present and active, both in their collective life and also as individuals.

My own story includes precisely this aspect. People helped orient me towards Jesus. Office workers making casual conversation over pastries, authors retelling their experience of God, others engaging my questions, the man in Leicester Square penning me a note, my friend who prayed with me afterwards, the group I met with for food and discussion, and the bookseller who always welcomed our visits—these are only the opening lines of a far longer list. Coming home to God is a personal and individual choice. But it is never *only* that. Jesus was explicit in his expectation that we would encounter God, in part, through others, as they tell us their stories and those of him and make tangible for us the reality of life with him.[101]

You may wish to take your next steps towards God in a similar fashion: by simply conversing over drinks with a friend who would say they know him. Sharing your half-formed thoughts and experiences, listening to theirs, playing with your questions and doubts. Or you might slide towards more structured contexts. Perhaps joining a course designed to help people contemplate God for the first time, like the popular Alpha, or Christianity Explored, which each run in most cities and towns, and provide a relaxed, safe space in which to discuss these things—nearly all participants at an Alpha or Christianity Explored are themselves just beginning to think it through.[102] Or Uncover, a simpler lo-fi equivalent, which takes place on university campuses around the UK and consists of open discussions around passages from the life of Jesus.[103] Maybe you could even dip a toe in the waters by visiting a couple of local churches or asking their leaders to chat over coffee.[104] Treading closer in the company of people.

God invites a response from us. The humbling reality, though, is that we are not the first people to receive such overtures. Our stories may each be unique, but it is often through others that we first glimpse the possibility of "something more" moving from notes on a page to live performance. Alongside other people is where the process of getting to know "God with us" unfolds—our personal and collective lives interweaving as we learn to be at home with our Creator and one another.

Inching Closer

Your invitation, like mine, arrives through the words of a person. Only this time, it is not via a crumpled note from a dishevelled man in central London. Instead, this little book finds its way into your hands. It suggests that you live not in an indifferent universe, rooted in some distant discompassionate energy, but that the one on whom everything is contingent has always seen and heard you, even when you weren't looking or listening, and that he has made himself known in the life of Jesus, who said to ordinary people like us, "I have called you friends".[105]

You are now holding this invitation in your hands. You could, of course, just file it away in a mental folder labelled "Curiosities". Archive it under "Enticing" or "Weird". Possibly both. Or you can respond. You have to start somewhere, so why not here? In a quiet place, away from others' ears—the car, the bedroom, in a park, even just whispered in the corner of a café, street, or bus—you could speak to whoever or whatever is out there. Praying, as I did, with your ordinary words and thoughts.

You could begin with Jesus' name. Not as a magic formula or incantation but simply to indicate that you are addressing him and speaking in response to all that is suggested by his story: his warmth of welcome, self-breaking forgiveness, and willingness to become a part of your everyday. Your words towards him can be candid and straightforward. Maybe a statement as simple as "I don't know if you're real, and I feel crazy even doing this, but if you are there, please guide me to the truth". There is no set formula for responding to God, except that we do so with honesty and openness. God is notoriously unshockable, and he can handle our deepest frustrations and sincerest misgivings.

You may even decide on bolder prayers, along the lines of "I want to come home to you. Please forgive me for the ways I resist you, and help me to learn what life looks like with you." Jesus once said that "whoever comes to me I will never drive away," and we can still take him up on that promise.[106] Perhaps by borrowing this prayer adapted from the words of novelist Dostoyevsky and asking:

"Please, here and now, could a new story begin: of my gradual renewal and gradual rebirth, of my gradual crossing from one world to another, of my acquaintance with your new, as yet unknown reality. I acknowledge that you are God, and I am not, and I

welcome you; please receive me and forgive me, and, as you promised, never drive me away."[107]

Opening this fresh tab in a long ongoing conversation, we become one of many who have responded to him, and it is alongside these others that we can explore our questions, be they intellectual or just practical. Together we can discover what it means for our general sense of something more to give way to a specific experience of him—no longer simply fluttering wings at the periphery of our vision but an increasingly integrated part of our ordinary lives.

Not everything will come into focus. Our finite imaginations can never fully grasp the one who is the source of all else. Nor need they do so. When an alert sounds or vibrates on our devices, suggesting a meeting or activity, our decision to ignore or respond is not based on exhaustive knowledge of the sender. Instead, we act from what we do know—that the person inviting us is, perhaps, one with whom we would like to spend time: to converse, to know and be known, to have alongside us in particular locations and times. That they would call us a friend and that we might say the same of them.

>Pause and Consider (or Discuss)

1. What would you like to say to God? If you were to pray to him right now, what would be the content of an honest and open response on your part?

2. What threads still hang loose for you? What would be your biggest questions related to the themes covered in this book?

3. With whom might you take your next steps? With which person might you arrange to have a conversation? And which communities or courses might you visit—do any spring to mind or will you need to do an online search or ask a friend for a recommendation?

Exploring Further

Other than contacting friends, visiting church communities near you, or praying, here are a few ways to move forward.

Read one or two of the original biographies of Jesus. Mark and Luke, both found in the New Testament, are an excellent starting point and are short and easy to read. A number of English translations of these stories (from the original Greek) are available, which combine accuracy with accessibility.

The two I tend to read are the New International Version and the New Living Translation. These are available from most bookshops, online at sites like Bible Gateway and Bible Hub, or via the Bible App from Life.Church. All these sites and apps also have a range of non-English language options, as well as other English translations. The app also has a free audio version, making it easy to listen while driving or walking.

Watch The Chosen: an excellent film adaptation of the life of Jesus, available to view online for free at: https://watch.angelstudios.com/thechosen/watch.

Enrol on a course like Alpha, Christianity Explored or—if you're a student—Uncover. There are plenty of others you could choose too. Just visit their websites to find out where one is running near you:

- Alpha: https://alpha.org

- Uncover: https://www.uncover.org.uk/

- Christianity Explored and Hope Explored: https://www.christianityexplored.org/

Read a book further exploring the themes of this book, such as:

- *Surprised by Joy*, the autobiography of C.S. Lewis, writer of the Narnia series, which vividly tells of his experience of God while an Oxford University tutor.

- *The Hiding Place* by Corrie ten Boom, which is the memoir of a Dutch woman living during the Nazi occupation and traces God's work during this dark period.

- *Unapologetic* by novelist and journalist Francis Spufford—a punchy and entertaining discussion of why God still makes surprising emotional sense.

- *Questioning Christianity* by Australian authors Daniel Paterson and Rian Roux, which explores some of the more intellectual questions and objections around the understanding of God presented in this book.

- *The Prodigal God* by Timothy Keller, which delves into one of Jesus' most famous stories and unpacks its meaning and relevance for today.

Notes on Using the End of Chapter Questions

You'll observe, as you go through *Somethingism*, that the book includes three questions at the end of each chapter. The aim of these questions is to enable further reflection on the possible connections between the book's content and your own life and experience. There's no real set way to use these, but—in case it's helpful—I thought I'd sketch out some suggested ways you *might* incorporate them into your own reading, or into a group discussion context.

First, if you're reading this book on your own, you could simply pause for a few moments after each question to crystallise your own thoughts. Even jot down some things on paper or a screen if that's your way of processing. I find it helpful to do my reflection in a quieter place, away from distractions—on a chair in the garden or on a short walk near our house. It may also help to have your phone on silent and tucked away, buying a few moments of focus.

If, on the other hand, you are reading *Somethingism* with another person or as part of a book group, then perhaps the questions could be used as a starting point for conversation when you meet. Each question could kick off a segment of conversation before moving on to the next, providing a shape to the discussion. Perhaps, as you read the book ahead of meeting together, you could also jot down your own questions that you might want to raise, and those can be thrown into the conversational mix.

The pace at which I have imagined groups discussing *Somethingism* is across four sessions, with everyone reading two chapters at a time and then coming together to discuss, before moving on to the next pair of chapters. Obviously, this pacing may not work for all groups, but hopefully the questions provide a starting point for whatever approach you decide to use.

Endnotes

EPIGRAPH

The quotations which open this book come from: Borges, Jorge Luis. *Selected Poems*. (London: Penguin, 2000), 43; Halík, Tomáš. *Patience with God: The Story of Zacchaeus Continuing in Us*. (New York: Doubleday, 2009), 114-115.

PREFACE

1 "Somethingism" has Dutch origins; it is an English translation of the word *ietsisme*, a term coined to describe the conviction, common among many in the Netherlands, that "there must be something" transcendent—a position more defined than the broader category of agnosticism. See, for example: Fallon, Francis and Gavin Hyman. *Agnosticism: Explorations in Philosophy and Religious Thought* (Oxford: Oxford University Press, 2020), 119-137; Boeve, Lieven. 2008. "Religion after Detraditionalization: Christian Faith in Post-Secular Europe." In *The New Visibility of Religion: Studies in Religion and Cultural Hermeneutics*, edited by Michael Hoelzl and Graham Ward, 187-209. (London: Continuum, 2008); Gan, Peter. 2022. "Is There Something Worthwhile in Somethingism." *European Journal for Philosophy of Religion*, 14 (4): 171-193.

CHAPTER ONE

2 "All men are created equal" comes from the United States Declaration of Independence: *U.S. Declaration of Independence and The Constitution of the United States.* (London: Penguin, 2012), 2. "The history of all hitherto existing society is the history of class struggles" is found in: Marx, Karl & Engels, Friedrich. *The Communist Manifesto.* (London: Penguin, 2004), 3. The third quote is slightly modified from "I have a dream that my four little children will one day live in a nation where they will not be judged by the color of their skin but by the content of their character", which comes from: King Jr., Martin Luther. *I Have a Dream.* (New York: HarperCollins, 2022), 70.

3 "Be true to yourself" and "Follow your heart" are the themes of innumerable films and plays, and some variation of them has been said in many works, dating at least back to Polonius' advice "to thine own self be true", given to his departing son in Shakespeare's *Hamlet* (Ham. 1.3.564). "One day my love will come" is a play on the line "Someday my prince will come", coined by lyricist Larry Morey and featured in: Hand, David, supervising dir. *Snow White and the Seven Dwarfs.* (Walt Disney Productions, 1937).

4 These are all popular online quotations, albeit none—from what I can ascertain—seems to have actually been said by the person with whom it is popularly associated. "Don't cry because it finished, smile because it happened" is often attributed to Dr. Seuss but doesn't appear in any of his published works. "It always seems impossible until it's done" is frequently ascribed to Nelson Mandela and, similarly, does not seem to be recorded in any official sources. "The key to success is failure" has probably been said by many people but is currently most commonly credited to basketball legend Michael Jordan, and seems to resonate with

his public statements, such as the Nike commercial 9,000 Shots, where he speaks these words, scripted for him by Jamie Barrett: "I've missed more than 9,000 shots in my career. I've lost almost 300 games. 26 times, I've been trusted to take the game winning shot and missed. I've failed over and over and over again in my life. And that is why I succeed." From: Romanek, Mark, dir. *9,000 Shots* (Propaganda Films, 1997).

5 See, for example: Polanyi, Michael. *Personal Knowledge: Towards a Post-Critical Philosophy*. (London: Routledge, 2005). Polanyi was a polymath, ranging across academic fields including chemistry, economics, and philosophy.

6 Comparison used throughout: Meek, Esther. *Longing to Know: The Philosophy of Knowledge for Ordinary People*. (Grand Rapids: Brazos, 2006).

7 Shakespeare's character Hamlet, in: Ham. 1.5.187-188.

8 The thoughts in this paragraph are borrowed from: Buechner, Frederick. *Secrets in the Dark: A Life in Sermons*. (New York: HarperOne, 2007), 16-21.

9 Murdoch, Iris. *The Sovereignty of Good*. (London: Routledge, 2001), 86.

10 He writes on this topic at length. See, for example: Galilei, Galileo. *Selected Writings*. (Oxford: Oxford University Press, 2012), 77, 115.

11 I Choose People, "Regina Spektor talks about belief and religion," YouTube, June 2, 2012, https://www.youtube.com/watch?v=Dnh2cBBTVlQ (accessed May 24, 2024).

12 Halík, Tomáš. *From the Underground Church to Freedom*. (Indiana: University of Notre Dame Press, 2019), 11. "Somethingism", as

noted in an endnote above, has older Dutch origins. It is unclear whether Halík arrived at the term independently or was aware of the Dutch concept before using it.

13 Dawkins, Richard. *River Out of Eden: A Darwinian View of Life.* (New York: Basic Books, 1995), 133.

CHAPTER TWO

14 My thanks to Matthew Cresswell for this story. I slightly adapted the quote to make it more accessible for international readers. The original, as recounted to me by Matthew, is "I'd say I believe, but it's like trying to get Virgin Radio when you're driving through the Chilterns—sometimes you can get it, and sometimes you can't, and you're just left twiddling the knob."

15 According to the Jewish and Christian scriptures, God made humankind in his image (Genesis 1:27). It is often observed that we then returned the favour.

16 Each of the people listed here has been open about their own perspective on God. Here is a little about each of them, together with a few exemplary quotes:

Donna Tartt, the acclaimed novelist, says that long-form fiction is an opportunity to explore questions of God without explicitly naming him. She writes, "A good novel … enables non-believers to participate in a world-view that religious people take for granted: life as a vast polymorphous web of interconnections, predestined meetings, fortuitous choices and accidents, all governed by a unifying if unforeseen plan."

Marilynne Robinson, Pulitzer Prize-winning novelist and essayist, weaves questions of God throughout her books. In one of her novels, she has a character say, "It [previously] seemed to me sometimes as though the Lord breathes on this poor gray ember of Creation and it turns to radiance for a moment or a year or the span of a life. And then it sinks back into itself again, and to look at it no one would know it had anything to do with fire, or light ... But the Lord is more constant and far more extravagant than [this]. Wherever you turn your eyes the world can shine ... You don't have to bring a thing to it except a little willingness to see. Only, who could have the courage to see it?"

Kizzmekia Corbett, an immunologist who teaches at Harvard University, and Francis Collins, former Director of the Human Genome Project, worked together on developing the Moderna vaccine for COVID-19. Collins told an interviewer, "I don't see that any of the issues that people raise as points of contention between science and faith are all that difficult to resolve ... I think God gave us an opportunity through the use of science to understand the natural world ... If God chose to create you and me ... and decided to use the mechanism of evolution to accomplish that goal, I think that's incredibly elegant."

Makoto Fujimura, a painter and author who draws on the Japanese Nihonga tradition, writes, "Our failure is not that we chose earth over heaven: it is that we fail to see the divine in the earth, already active and working, pouring forth grace and spilling glory into our lives. Artists, whether they are professed believers or not, tap into this grace and glory."

Lauren Daigle's songs, which have been streamed billions of times via online services such as Pandora and Spotify, frequently explore the theme of God, and are even addressed to him. Her 2018 album *Look Up Child* is a good starting point for exploring her work.

Sources: Tartt, Donna. 2000. "The spirit and writing in a

secular world." In *The Novel, Spirituality and Modern Culture: Eight Novelists write about their Craft and Context*, edited by Paul Fiddes, 37-38. (Cardiff: University of Wales Press, 2000); Robinson, Marilynne. *Gilead*. (London: Virago, 2004), 280; "Interview with Francis Collins." PBS, 2004, https://www.pbs.org/wgbh/questionofgod/voices/collins.html. (accessed July 31, 2024); Fujimura, Makoto. *Silence and Beauty: Hidden Faith Born of Suffering* (Downers Grove: InterVarsity Press, 2016), 89; Daigle, Lauren. Look Up Child. Centricity Music, 2018.

17 The book I'm referencing here in my story is by John Stott. It pointed me towards the specific portrait of the transcendent discussed in chapters 3 to 8 of this book: Stott, John. *The Incomparable Christ*. (Leicester: Inter-Varsity Press, 2001).

18 This current section zooms out from the specific view of God discussed by Stott to the wider (epistemological) questions it raised for me, then and subsequently. This section's contours have been especially shaped by: Hart, David Bentley. *The Experience of God*. (New Haven: Yale University Press, 2013); Shortt, Rupert. *God Is No Thing*. (London: C.Hurst & Co, 2016). I return to the perspective Stott and I share in the following chapters.

19 A version of this and the following diagram first appeared in one of my previous books: Cawley, Luke. *The Myth of the Non-Christian: Engaging Atheists, Nominal Christians and the Spiritual but Not Religious*. (Downers Grove: InterVarsity Press, 2016), 124-126.

20 See his interview, here: Lewis, Helen. "If we could prove string theory wrong, I would be thrilled!" *New Statesman*, June 11, 2011, http://www.newstatesman.com/blogs/helen/lewis-hasteley/2011/06/physics-theory-ideas-universe (accessed June 18, 2024).

21 Cretan philosopher Epimenides and the apostle Paul, as cited in and from Acts 17:27-28.

22 These figures would be supported by almost any source on this topic. These would include the well-regarded CIA World Factbook, https://www.cia.gov/the-world-factbook/field/religions (accessed June 18, 2024); and "Population Growth Projections, 2010–2050", Pew Research Forum, April 2, 2015, https://www.pewresearch.org/religion/2015/04/02/religious-projections-2010-2050 (accessed June 18, 2024).

Sometimes people are surprised that Sikhism and Judaism are not on this list, but each constitutes a relatively small (<0.3%) segment of the global population, with higher concentrations in limited geographical areas. If they were added to this list, for whatever reason, it wouldn't alter the basic point of this section—that the number of widespread options which exhibit extensive transnational and transethnic appeal remains relatively small, and at odds with the assumption that we are drowning in thousands of possibilities.

23 When I'm asked what all religions have in common, I sometimes reply "antireductionism". "Reductionism", in this context, meaning "reducing" life down to the material and physical, a move which the major religions resist—hence they can be said to possess a shared antireductionism. As this book's title, *Somethingism*, suggests, even many without religious affiliation or commitment have antireductionist—or somethingist—instincts. We all, it seems, share much more in common than we typically assume.

But on the specific question of God (by which I mean the idea that the something on which the universe is contingent has a mind and will), there is variety of views among the seven on my list:

- Atheism obviously denies God's existence, while "agnosticism" is the term for those without any fixed view.

- Buddhism also doesn't ordinarily touch on the question of God. Most forms of Buddhism actually deny the existence of a God. This often surprises Western people, especially those who assume that all religions are the same.

- Most streams within the last five on the list (Hinduism, Chinese traditional religion, African traditional religion, Islam, and Christianity) do include some emphasis on God.

The key variation in terms of how these latter five approach God isn't in relation to his existence so much as it is to the question of if and how he may have revealed himself to us, and—consequently—what this communicates about his character and how we might relate to him.

The theme of God's possible self-revelation is one we will pick up in chapter 3 with a wide lens, and then again in chapter 4 with a closer focus on one particular claim to self-revelation, the implications of which we explore for the remainder of the book.

Notes on the above: The atheist philosopher Thomas Nagel first highlighted to me the helpfulness of the term "antireductionism", which he uses several times in: Nagel, Thomas. *Mind and Cosmos: Why the Materialist Neo-Darwinian Conception of Nature Is Almost Certainly False.* (Oxford: Oxford University Press, 2012).

With regards to Buddhism being ordinarily non-theistic, an easy starting place for this is: Keown, Daniel. *Buddhism: A Very Short Introduction.* (Oxford: Oxford University Press, 2013), 5. It has been mooted that perhaps certain strands of Buddhism (for example, Mahāyāna Buddhism) may have a theistic (or God-themed) element, by another name, as discussed in: Davide

Andrea Zappulli, "Towards a Buddhist Theism," *Religious Studies* 59, no. 4 (December 2023): 762–74; Paul Knitter and Peter Feldmeier, "Are Buddhism and Christianity Commensurable? A Debate/Dialogue Between Paul Knitter and Peter Feldmeier," *Buddhist-Christian Studies* 36 (2016): 165–84. There is also an explicit concept of God as "Sanghyang Adi Buddha", which has become (controversially) widespread in Indonesian Buddhism, described in: Brown, Iem "Contemporary Indonesian Buddhism and Monotheism," *Journal of Southeast Asian Studies* 18, no. 1 (1987): 108–17; Obuse, Kieko, "Finding God in Buddhism: A New Trend in Contemporary Buddhist Approaches to Islam," *Numen* 62, no. 4 (2015): 408–30. So even Buddhism isn't entirely outside the God discussion, even if most forms are conventionally described as non-theistic.

My point, though, in this second chapter (and these endnotes) is not to forge a critique of various religions or to make an argument for one against the others but simply to suggest that it's helpful to start with particular claims to revelation, among which this book focuses on one.

24 From the poem "Vowels and Sirens", in: Lewis, C.S. *Poems*. (New York: HarperOne, 2017), 118.

25 For example: Halík, Tomáš, *Patience with God: The Story of Zacchaeus Continuing in Us*. (New York: Doubleday, 2009), ix.

CHAPTER THREE

26 John 14:9; 10:30. The exact original phrasing was "Anyone who has seen me has seen the Father" and "I and the Father are one". Jesus was here using the language of "Father" for God, which is how his first listeners understood its meaning and is how Jesus used the term—see, for example, how he told his followers to

begin their prayers with "Our Father" (Matthew 6:9). I have sought to make this clearer for present-day readers who may be less familiar with the context.

27 The four key accounts of Jesus' life, based on eyewitness testimony, are usually referred to as Matthew, Mark, Luke and John. After their writing and distribution, they came to form a part of the New Testament, which is itself a collection of documents from the first decades after Jesus' life. Christians treat these texts as the key resource for making sense of God, though one doesn't need to make such a commitment in order to begin enjoying them—readers of all persuasions find them accessible and thought-provoking. Though originally written in Greek, they are now available in a range of contemporary English translations, including as written texts, audiobooks, and filmed adaptations. More details on easy ways to access and enjoy these biographies of Jesus today are listed in the Exploring Further section at the end of this book. The remainder of this book also focuses on some of the themes and contours of these texts.

28 John 10:9, RSV.

29 Jesus' status in Islam is well-known. Two books which touch on this, by a Christian and a Muslim respectively, are: Shumack, Richard. *Jesus through Muslim Eyes*. (London: SPCK, 2020); Siddiqui, Mona. *Christians, Muslims, and Jesus*. (New Haven: Yale University Press, 2013).

Jesus as bodhisattva and as avatar are also common concepts, though Jesus is not a codified element of the relevant religions in the way he is in Islam, and so views on him vary among Hindus and Buddhists. The Dalai Lama—the Tibetan Buddhist leader—says that "for me, as a Buddhist, my attitude towards Jesus Christ is that he was either a fully enlightened being or a bodhisattva of a very high spiritual realisation", as recorded in: The Dalai Lama, *The Good Heart: A Buddhist Perspective on the Teachings of Jesus* (Boston: Wisdom Publications, 1998), 83. Influential Indian Hindu yogi and philosopher Sri Aurobindo calls Jesus "the avatar of sorrow and suffering", as recorded in: Gregory A. Barker and Stephen E. Gregg, *Jesus Beyond Christianity: The Classic Texts* (Oxford: OUP Oxford, 2010), 193.

30 Painter Frida Kahlo seems to have incorporated imagery traditionally associated with Jesus into her work, including a nod to the crown of thorns in *Self-Portrait with Thorn Necklace and Hummingbird* (1940, oil on canvas, Harry Ransom Center, Austin, Texas), the sacred heart in *Las dos Fridas* (1939, oil on canvas, Museo de Arte Moderno, Mexico City), the Last Supper in *The Wounded Table* (1940, oil on wood, lost), and the crucifixion in *The Broken Column* (1944, oil on Masonite, Museo Dolores Olmedo, Mexico City).

Historian and philosopher Hannah Arendt, most famous for her first-hand description of and reflections on the trial of Nazi war criminal Adolf Eichmann, repeatedly discussed Jesus in her works, including in: Arendt, Hannah. *Responsibility and Judgement.* (New York: Schocken, 2003), 111-112, 274; Arendt, Hannah. *Men in Dark Times* (New York: Harvest/HBJ, 1968), 58-59; Arendt, Hannah. *The Human Condition.* (Chicago: University of Chicago Press, 1998).

Novelists Philip Pullman and José Saramago wrote fictional works about Jesus which both diverge enormously from the historical narrative: Pullman, Philip. *The Good Man Jesus and the Scoundrel Christ.* (Edinburgh: Canongate, 2017); Saramago, José. *The Gospel According to Jesus Christ.* (London: Vintage, 2008).

31 Jesus was Jewish, and he initiated a renewal movement within

Judaism, which later became known as Christianity. His first followers were all Jewish. Over time the two movements, Judaism and Christianity, developed separate identities, albeit with a continued substantial overlap—not least because the Jewish scriptures are also included in the Christian scriptures, where they are commonly referred to as the Old Testament, or First Testament. Many Christians today are also Jewish, recognising Jesus as the Messiah of the Jewish scriptures, though the Christian movement globally is now ethnically much broader than it was at the beginning, encompassing many thousands of (non-Jewish) people groups. The list of countries with the most professing Christians in the world currently includes Mexico, the United States, Brazil, the Philippines, China, Nigeria, D.R. Congo, Russia, Germany, and Ethiopia. See: Diamant, Jeff. "The Countries with the 10 Largest Christian Populations and the 10 Largest Muslim Populations," Pew Research Center, April 1, 2019, https://www.pewresearch.org/short-reads/2019/04/01/the-countries-with-the-10-largest-christian-populations-and-the-10-largest-muslim-populations/. (accessed June 18, 2024).

32 Paraphrased quotation. The original reads, "There is enough light for those whose only desire is to see, and enough darkness for those of the opposite disposition". From: Pascal, Blaise. *Pensées and Other Writings*. (Oxford: Oxford University Press, 2008), 81.

33 Robinson, Marilynne. *Gilead*. (London: Virago, 2004), 280.

CHAPTER FOUR

34 Jesus, contrary to the events depicted in most school Nativity plays, was probably born in the house of relatives. Mary and Joseph were in Bethlehem because the Roman emperor had called for a census and people had to return to register in

the places of their birth; so Joseph likely had relatives there. This region, then and now, was a hospitable one, and it is inconceivable that a couple, one of whom was pregnant, could arrive in a place where the husband had relatives, or a family history, and be left on the streets, trawling around the doorways of strangers in search of a room.

Many houses would have had a guest room, and this was "the inn" where there was no space. The original Greek word sometimes translated into English as "inn" (*katalyma*) denotes this spare room; the author would have used a different word (*pandocheion*) instead had they been referring to a commercial inn (see Bailey, below). Most modern English translations of the text now read "no guest room [was] available for them" (NIV) or "no lodging available for them" (NLT). This all indicates that the point of the "no room in the inn" is to communicate that Jesus was probably born in the main shared family room rather than in the guest room (Luke 2:7).

Hence there being no references to animals in the early narratives of Jesus: he wasn't in a barn at all. It was common practice for animals to be brought into the spare room at night, and there would either have been straw placed within a depression in the floor or a wooden manger for them to eat from. This manger could have been moved to the main family room, and this is probably "the manger" where he was laid.

As Ian Paul comments, "The belief that Jesus was lonely and dejected, cast out amongst the animals and sidelined at his birth, actually seriously distorts the meaning of the birth narratives, in which ... Jesus and his birth are a powerfully disruptive force, bursting in on the middle of ordinary life and offering the possibility of its transformation."

For a fuller account: Bailey, Kenneth. *Jesus through Middle Eastern Eyes*. (Downers Grove: InterVarsity Press, 2016), 25-37. Bailey's book has some helpful diagrams of local architecture and how rooms were laid out. See also: Paul, Ian. "Jesus wasn't born in a stable—and that makes all the difference," *Psephizo*, November 30, 2020, https://www.psephizo.com/biblical-studies/jesus-wasnt-born-in-a-stable-and-that-makes-all-the-difference (accessed June 25, 2024).

35 The entire opening section of this chapter draws on the original 1st-century accounts of Jesus' life, and the elements mentioned here can be found in the references below:

- Escaping a massacre under cover of darkness and a period as refugees: Matthew 2:13-21.
- His mother's song: Luke 1:46-56.
- Carpenter, son of a carpenter: Mark 6:3; Matthew 13:55. The word usually translated as "carpenter" in English actually covers a wider range of manual labour, including stonemasonry. So it is slightly ambiguous whether he worked in wood, stone or both.
- John's fiery speeches to the crowds: Luke 3:1-19.
- John arrested and executed: Luke 3:19-20; 7:18-25; 9:9; Mark 1:14; 6:17-29; Matthew 11:2-8; 14:6-12.
- John designates Jesus as the chosen one: John 1:26-36.
- Jesus disappears for a month: Luke 4:1-13; Matthew 4:1-11; John 1:35-51.
- Family seem less than impressed: John 7:5.
- Indignation of neighbours: Mark 6:3; Matthew 13:55-57.
- Synagogue speech, subsequent riot and an attempt to throw him off a cliff: Luke 4:14-28.
- Jesus gathers followers: Matthew 4:18-22; Mark 1:16-20; Luke 5:1-11.

- Small local businessmen: Peter and Andrew were fishermen, according to Matthew 4:18-22, Mark 1:16-20 and Luke 5:1-11.
- Dodgy civil servant: Matthew, one of Jesus' disciples, was—prior to meeting Jesus—a tax collector, and as such would have been viewed as a hated collaborator with the occupying Romans. See Matthew 9:9; 10:3.
- Member of revolutionary terrorist band: Simon, one of Jesus' disciples, is described as a "Zealot", which was one belonging to a political movement that agitated for an armed uprising against Rome. See Matthew 10:4, Mark 3:18, Luke 6:15 and Acts 1:13.

- Accents of Jesus' followers and the reactions they invoked: Acts 2:7.
- Interactions with...
  - those seen as immoral or untrustworthy: Luke 19:5-7.
  - those crushed by the system: John 9:1-34.
  - those burdened by life: John 4:1-26.
- Turning out in their thousands: Matthew 14:13-21; 15:29-39; Mark 8:1-13; Luke 9:14.
- Touching those with infectious skin diseases: Matthew 8:2-3.
- Welcoming local sex workers to the dining table: Luke 7:36-39; 15:1-2.
- Stories about...
  - building projects: Luke 12:13-21; 14:28-30.
  - lost possessions: Luke 15:1-10.
  - agricultural practices: Matthew 13:1-23; Mark 4:1-20; Luke 8:1-15.
  - family breakdowns: Luke 15:11-32.
  - shady employers: Luke 16:1-13.
- Prediction of his own demise and the assumption that it was a metaphor: Mark 9:9-10; Matthew 20:17-28.

- Riding on a donkey: Matthew 21:1-11; Luke 19:28-44; John 12:12-19.
- The ancient piece of literature this donkey ride references: Zechariah 9:9-10, which was part of the Jewish scriptures and a well-known text in the time and context, making these actions unmistakable in their intent.
- Marching into the temple and smashing it up: Matthew 21:12-17; Mark 11:15-19; Luke 19:45-48; John 2:13-16.
- Arrest and the manoeuvres behind it: Matthew 26:14-16, 47-56; 27:1-10.
- Lies and abandonment: Matthew 26:47-75.
- Popular vote: Matthew 27:15-26; Mark 15:6-15; Luke 23:13-25; John 18:33-40.
- Execution: Matthew 27:27-66.

36 This and the following sentence rework two lines from scholar Kenneth Bailey and owe their content, shape and a number of word choices to: Bailey, Kenneth. *Jesus through Middle Eastern Eyes*. (Downers Grove: InterVarsity Press, 2016), 279.

37 Crane, Stephen. *The Complete Poems*. (New York: Honeycomb Press, 2011), 110.

38 NPR Staff, "Christopher Hitchens on Suffering, Beliefs and Dying," NPR, October 29, 2010, https://www.npr.org/2010/10/29/130917506/christopher-hitchens-on-suffering-beliefs-and-dying (accessed August 28, 2024).

39 Watterson, Bill. *The Complete Calvin and Hobbes: Book Three*. (Kansas City: Andrews McMeel, 2006), 247.

40 Tolkien, J.R.R. *The Hobbit*. (London: HarperCollins, 2013), 15.

41 Schaeffer, Francis. *True Spirituality*. (Wheaton: Tyndale, 2001), 35.

42 John 1:9.

43 Phrase borrowed from Alan Hirsch, who used it during a class at which the author was present, at Wheaton College Graduate School in 2011.

44 Tennyson, Alfred. *The Complete Poems*. (New York: B. Worthington, 1878), 224.

45 NavPress, "Peterson: In Between the Man and the Message," YouTube, August 30, 2016, https://www.youtube.com/watch?v=LaMgIvbXqSk (accessed August 22, 2014). See also: Peterson, Eugene. *Holy Luck: Poems*. (Grand Rapids: Eerdmans, 2013), 45.

46 Newton, John. *Olney Hymns, in Three Books*. (London: W. Oliver, 1821), 53.

CHAPTER FIVE

47 Luke 19:28-44; 23:1-56.

48 Luke 23:21.

49 Luke 4:14-30.

50 Luke 4:22.

51 Luke 4:29.

52 Rosanna Greenstreet, "Q&A: Phil Daniels," *The Guardian*, July 12, 2014, https://www.theguardian.com/lifeandstyle/2014/jul/12/phil-daniels-interview (accessed August 1, 2024).

53 Nagel, Thomas. *The Last Word*. (Oxford: Oxford University Press, 1997), 130.

54 Thompson, Francis. *The Hound of Heaven and Other Poems*. Boston: (International Pocket Library, 2000), 11.

55 Lewis, C.S. *Perelandra*. (London: HarperCollins, 2005), 15.

56 Matthew 11:17, ESV.

57 Lewis, C.S. *Perelandra*. (London: HarperCollins, 2005), 15.

58 Auden, W.H. *New Year Letter*. (London: Faber and Faber, 1941), 119.

59 This is my precis of the following section in Halík's book: "If our reason (or more precisely, modern rationality) leaves us in a state of uncertainty, then we can ask ourselves the simple but cardinal question, Do I want God to be or not to be? This question awaits an answer from the profoundest depth of our hearts, from the very core of our being. Perhaps the answer to this question is far more important than our answer to the question that people ask us, that is, our opinion about whether or not God exists. If someone answers that they don't know whether God exists, that need not conclude their reflection on God. They can ask another question: Do I yearn for him? Do I want God to be?" From: Halík, Tomáš, *I Want You to Be: On the God of Love*. (Indiana: University of Notre Dame Press, 2016), 63.

60 Matthew 9:4.

CHAPTER SIX

61 Cuarón, Alfonso, dir. *Gravity*. (Warner Bros Pictures, 2013).

62 Solzhenitsyn, Aleksandr. *The Gulag Archipelago 1918-1956: An Experiment in Literary Investigation III-IV*. (New York: Harper & Row, 1973), 615.

63 John Crowley, dir., *The Goldfinch* (Warner Bros., 2019); originally a quote from Francois de La Rochefoucauld—"We are so much accustomed to disguise ourselves to others, that at length we

disguise ourselves to ourselves", he writes in: de La Rochefoucauld, Francis. *Moral Reflections, Sentences and Maxims of Francois, Duc de La Rochefoucauld.* (New York: William Gowans, 1851), 39. It is also cited in the book from which the film is adapted: Tartt, Donna. *The Goldfinch.* (London: Abacus, 2014), 417.

64 Luke 23:34.

65 Jesus, in this prayer says, "Forgive them, for they do not know what they are doing". And few of us really know what we are doing when it comes to God, but it's interesting that Jesus sees those with an unknowing self-distancing from God as still in need of reconciliatory forgiveness. This makes sense: we can all take actions which cause relational ruptures without being cognisant of doing so. It's also notable that he doesn't require us to fully comprehend him or ourselves in order to have forgiveness made available to us. "Forgive them, for they do not know what they are doing" expresses his stance towards all of us who understand (at best) very little of God.

66 See: Kitamori, Kazoh. *Theology of the Pain of God.* (Eugene: Wipf & Stock, 2005).

67 *Time.* 2021. Series 1, episodes 1-3. Directed by Lewis Arnold. Aired June 6, 2021, on BBC iPlayer. https://www.bbc.co.uk/iplayer/episodes/p09fs2qh/time.

68 Luke 22:19.

69 Mark 10:45.

CHAPTER SEVEN

70 Apparently he didn't fully register the sharks until the moments of his rescue; his energies were absorbed in avoiding imminent

drowning by disentangling himself.

71 Cruz, Nicky, with Jamie Buckingham. *Run Baby Run.* (London: Hodder and Stoughton, 2010).

72 Colson, Charles. *Born Again.* (Grand Rapids: Chosen, 2008). Also: Colson, Charles. *Life Sentence.* (London: Hodder and Stoughton, 1980).

73 Wilkerson, David. *The Cross and the Switchblade.* (New York: Jove Books, 1977).

74 Cash writes that his "most serious and protracted" spell of drug use "began when I took painkillers after eye surgery in 1981, then kept taking them after I didn't need to. It escalated after I was almost killed by an ostrich", and then he goes on to tell the story. From: Cash, Johnny. *Cash: The Autobiography.* (London: Harper, 1997), 189.

75 Name changed.

76 In the interests of complete accuracy, I'll note here that we were eating something, and I recall it as a Danish pastry. Maybe it was something else.

77 John 1:28-29; 1:37-39; 2:1-11; 3:1-8; 4:4-6; 5:1-6; 6:5-13; 6:16-21; 7:1-24; 11:1-17; 12:1-2.

78 John 1:35-42; 3:1-21; 4:1-26, 46-54; 5:1-14; 11:17-44.

79 Cash, Johnny. 1970. "I'm A Free Man Now." *Guideposts*, (November 1970).

80 John 10:9, RSV.

81 My father's classification of himself as "a sceptic who believes" was partially a nod towards his own doubts. It was also a

description of how he had come to apply this scepticism towards his own previously agnostic assumptions. In short, he didn't see being a sceptical, questioning person with doubts as being in tension with experiencing and following Jesus.

82 Mark 9:24, ESV.

83 The Jewish scriptures, which are also part of the Christian Bible (as the "First Testament" or "Old Testament"), repeatedly place this simple prayer of "Here I am" on the lips of its protagonists, as their way of telling God exactly this. See, for example, Genesis 22:1, 11; 31:11; 46:2; Isaiah 6:8.

84 Revelation 4:10-11.

85 Dostoyevsky, Fyodor. *Crime and Punishment.* (London: Penguin, 2014), Kindle Locations 9827. I have very slightly adapted/paraphrased this quotation to make it gender inclusive.

CHAPTER EIGHT

86 Kierkegaard, Søren. *Either/Or Part I.* (New Jersey: Princeton University Press, 1987), 68. Italics mine.

87 Joel 2:22, from a chapter of ancient prophecy later cited by Peter, Jesus' close friend, in his first public address following the crucifixion. Peter used it as part of his interpretive grid for events then unfolding: Jesus' giving of the Holy Spirit as the one through whom Jesus empowers his followers.

88 MacDonald, George. *Poetical Works Volume II.* (London: Chatto & Windus, 1893), 362.

89 Skinner, Frank. *A Comedian's Prayer Book.* (London: Hodder & Stoughton, 2021), 5, Kindle.

90 Carson, Clayborne (ed.). *The Autobiography of Martin Luther King, Jr.* (New York: Warner Books, 2001), 78-79.

91 From a 1967 sermon, known as "But not if", as cited in: Rieder, Jonathan. *The Word of the Lord Is Upon Me: The Righteous Performance of Martin Luther King Jr.* (Cambridge: Harvard University Press, 2009), 124. Also included, and juxtaposed with the above incident, in: Carson, Clayborne (ed.). *The Autobiography of Martin Luther King, Jr.* (New York: Warner Books, 2001), 79.

King also asked every volunteer during this time to sign a "Commitment Card", with a set of ten pledges, the first of which was to "meditate daily on the life and teachings of Jesus": a request born from his conviction that it was in Jesus that they would hear the voice of God. See: King, Martin Luther. *Why We Can't Wait.* (London: Penguin, 2018), 69.

92 See, for example: John 1:1-5, 14; 1 John 1:1.

93 John 1:14, NRSV.

94 Mark and Luke, both found in the New Testament, are an excellent starting point. See the "Exploring Further" section, which follows chapter 8, for more details.

95 Matthew 1:23.

96 1 Corinthians 15:3-8. The chapter in which this text sits (1 Corinthians 15) is generally agreed to have been written around 20 years after Jesus' crucifixion and was part of a letter designed to be read aloud to a group of Jesus' followers in the city of Corinth. It is notable because of its assumptions that the resurrection and the number (and identity) of witnesses to it were common knowledge, which indicates how embedded the story of the resurrection had become within a very short

timeframe. Other earlier written references to the resurrection exist, but this one is perhaps the most striking.

97 A good starting point for considering science and God is a short, accessible book by an Oxford University mathematics professor: Lennox, John. *Can Science Explain Everything?* (Epsom: The Good Book Company, 2019).

98 Phrase adapted from C.S. Lewis' description of the lion Aslan's resurrection in one of the Narnia books: "The [White] Witch [should] have known that when a willing victim who had committed no treachery was killed in a traitor's stead, the Table would crack and Death itself would start working backwards". From: Lewis, C.S. *The Lion, the Witch and the Wardrobe*. (London: HarperCollins, 2009), 176.

99 It's beyond our current scope to further probe the historical dimension at length. But, in short, the story of Jesus' resurrection began circulating incredibly early and rapidly gained credibility in the very city where much of the populace had recently witnessed his execution. Imagine, in your town, that someone publicly murdered was soon thereafter said to be back—alive and in full health. It would require something incredible for that to gain traction. Even very sceptical contemporary historians, therefore, affirm that those making the claims were convinced of them. Many of the claimants went to their deaths for it, and it gained them no power or wealth. Yet no one seems to have recanted. No shrine site in veneration of the late, great Jesus emerged because there was no body to honour.

Here are a few resources to pick from if you want to read further:

- A readable introduction to historical questions around the earliest stories of Jesus is: Williams, Peter. *Can We Trust the Gospels?* (Wheaton: Crossway, 2019).

- Specifically on the resurrection, a good overview of its significance, as well as some treatment of the arguments for it, is: Keller, Timothy. *Hope in Times of Fear: The Resurrection and the Meaning of Easter.* (London: Hodder & Stoughton, 2021).

- If you're brave enough to take on an academic work of over 800 pages, then the seminal recent publication is: Wright, N.T. *The Resurrection of the Son of God.* (London: SPCK, 2017).

- A recent film based on the true story of someone looking into the historical evidence for Jesus is: Gunn, Jon, dir. *The Case for Christ.* (Pure Flix Entertainment, 2017).

100 Johnson, Luke Timothy. *Miracles: God's Presence and Power in Creation.* (Louisville: Westminster John Knox, 2018), 148.

101 Jesus gathered friends around him, whom we call "disciples". They learned to love God and live with him by spending time with Jesus. When Jesus was preparing to withdraw physically from the world, he told them to "make disciples" of others (Matthew 28:19). His plan, in other words, was for them to do with others exactly what he had done with them: spend time together, eat, share stories, and through this human interaction learn to perceive and experience God.

102 Find an Alpha or Christianity Explored near you, at: https://alpha.org or https://www.christianityexplored.org.

103 Details and videos at: https://www.uncover.org.uk.

104 Most churches list their meeting times and contact details on their social-media pages and websites. Just do an online search and see what's near you.

105 John 15:15.

106 John 6:37.

107 This prayer is mine, but it was adapted, augmented (with material from throughout this book, especially the statement "I am God, and you are not" from chapter 7, and Jesus' statement that "whoever comes to me I will never drive away"), and personalised from the same quotation used at the conclusion of the previous chapter and drawn from here: Dostoyevsky, Fyodor. *Crime and Punishment*. (London: Penguin, 2014), Kindle Location 9827.

Acknowledgements

This book draws on and further develops some of what I previously designed for the Passion Weeks: a series of week-long events on university campuses around the Netherlands, organised by IFES, with the constant involvement of Navigators, along with the regular support of Studentlife and Veritas Forum. It was also informed by the conversations and interactions which unfolded during and after these events. So, my thanks go to the students and staff in Delft, Groningen, Eindhoven and Amsterdam, and especially to my friend and *eierbal* consultant Frederik Boersema for inviting me to be part of it all.

It also flows from thinking and practice developed for Chrysolis's Engage project, primarily run in partnership with OSCER/IFES within Romania, though also encompassing a range of shorter partnership-based projects across the continent. Engage, like Passion Weeks, consists of structured discussions with university students, and I want to thank our friends in

OSCER/IFES—as well as the Chrysolis team over the years—for their role in helping make possible the many rich discussions which helped shape this book.

Despite this background in physical conversations and presentations, though, this little paperback is not a set of transcribed talks. It is, instead, the outcome of further developing that thinking and crafting it into a short piece of literature. Especially informing its style and approach are Wendell Berry and Frederik Buechner, for whose examples I am thankful.

People who have read (or listened to) either sections or the entirety of this book, and whose feedback has helped shape it, include Benedict Cambridge, Ann Cawley, Whitney Cawley, Ioana Gliția, Stephanie Heald, Kristi Mair, Caitlin Ormiston, Wes Poirot and Nigel Pollock. Thank you each for taking the time and for being part of *Somethingism*'s development.

Thank you also to Dan Ehrman, who had a brief cameo in the early stages of this book's path to publication, before it found its eventual destination. I am hugely thankful, Dan, for your generous willingness to advocate for the book, following my random message to you.

A note of appreciation goes to my editor, Rachel Jones, for her work during the process of bringing this to publication, and also to all within The Good Book Company involved in its production and development.

The time to craft a work like this, and to participate in conversations and events on which it draws, is made possible by those who support me in my current role. Thank you! Particular gratitude here goes to the Trustee Board of Chrysolis—Cait, Kristi, Stephen Humphries,

Trevor Raaff, and Hannah Giddings—who are such an enormous support and encouragement, in both challenging and smooth times.

My ability to stay sane in the writing process is partly down to the warmth and love of our family home, and most especially to the amazing Whitney, to whom this book is dedicated.

Our kids—Jackson, William and Amélie—have also brought energy, joy, humour and an (ahem!) diverse soundscape to our household throughout the writing of this book. I hope you enjoy seeing your names in print once again. You are each loved and appreciated for who you are!

And to the Someone who brings our sense of something into focus—thank you for life and breath and everything else.

thegoodbook
COMPANY

Thanks for reading this book. We hope you enjoyed it and found it helpful.

Most people want to find answers to the big questions of life: Who are we? Why are we here? How should we live? But we are often unable to find the time or space to think positively and carefully about them.

At The Good Book Company, we're passionate about producing resources that help people of all ages and stages to understand the heart of the Christian message, found in the pages of the Bible, and to see how that message provides answers to our biggest questions.

So whoever you are and wherever you are at, we hope we can help you to think things through. Visit our website to discover the range of books and other resources we publish, both for people who are looking into Christianity and those who have already made the decision to follow Jesus. Or head to our partner site at christianityexplored.org/what-is-christianity for a clear explanation of who Jesus is and why he came.

Thanks again for reading.

Your friends at The Good Book Company

thegoodbook.com | thegoodbook.co.uk
thegoodbook.com.au | thegoodbook.co.nz | thegoodbook.co.in

CHRISTIANITYEXPLORED.ORG

A great place to explore the Christian faith, with powerful testimonies and answers to difficult questions.